Praise for *Just As You Are*

A sincere, humble, and intimate record of the transformative encounter with Other Power. Satya and Kaspa deftly interweave stimulating reflections on Pure Land thought and history with poignant, personal testimonies that beckon us into a space of deepening awareness and profound connection.

– Nagapriya, author of *The Promise of a Sacred World: Shinran's Teaching of Other Power.*

This book offers a rich patchwork of articles sharing not just the fundamentals of Pure Land Buddhism, but also the lived experiences of practitioners. I particularly appreciate the way in which it interweaves the ground of ideas, practice and lifestyle with personal anecdotes from members of the Bright Earth group. Chapters by Satya and Kaspa include candid expositions of their own experiences on their spiritual journeys and of the evolving practice and organisation of their community, as well as setting out with clarity their current positioning as a thriving independent Buddhist community, feeling its way forwards. Drawing on roots of teaching from the Pure Land patriarchs of China and Japan, as well as recent teachers in a number of different Pure Land and other Buddhist traditions, the picture painted in this book is religiously well informed and at the same time deeply embedded in the real worlds of environmental action, psychological therapies and social action. I would certainly recommend this book to anyone wanting to know more in particular about the Bright Earth tradition, but also to those seeking to broaden their understanding of Buddhism in its breadth and depth.

– Caroline Brazier, Jodo Shinshu priest and author of *The Other Buddhism.*

I was a fan of the first edition of *Just As You Are: Buddhism For Foolish Beings* but I think the second edition really hits the sweet spot in explaining the form of Buddhism Kaspa and Satya practice in their temple. It continues to introduce readers to Pure Land Buddhism but with more detail about its history, and expanding beyond an introduction to Pure Land to include new spiritual influences from their study with Bright Dawn and the Reverends Gyomay and Koyo Kubose. Although I am prejudiced, as a Bright Dawn lay minister and Sensei, the practice of everyday Buddhism – bringing the Dharma into the everyday of our lives as delightful, foolish beings – feels like the backbone of this new edition. The reinforcing structure to the everyday Buddhism Kaspa and Satya present in this book is their deep commitment to engaged and ecological Buddhism. Their dedication to this three-fold structure of an everyday, engaged, and ecological Buddhism is a rare combination that answers the needs of the world right now with sound Buddhist teachings that they write about with a bright passion.

– Wendy Shinyo Haylett, founder & host of the podcast, *Everyday Buddhism: Making Everyday Better*, and author of *Everyday Buddhism: Real-Life Buddhist Teachings & Practices For Real Change.*

Just As You Are is a warm, accessible introduction to the practices of Pure Land Buddhism and a delightful glimpse into the life of two committed practitioners who not only teach the path, but live it. The writing is both honest and clear, personable and open, and it paints a compelling picture of the practices of Pure Land Buddhism and of temple living – or, short of that, of a life dedicated to the dharma. Satya and Kaspa are trustworthy guides, and those interested in exploring Pure Land Buddhism and its devotional practices would do well to entrust themselves to their guidance.

– Vanessa Zuisei Goddard, author of *Still Running: The Art of Meditation in Motion.*

What the authors have done in this book is show the way toward attentive compassion – compassion towards others but also, and maybe more importantly, towards oneself. I laughed out loud at the idea of the validation of our foolish, bombu nature.

The introduction to daily practice is succinct and blessedly clear. The book uses the upaya of personal experience to draw one in to the value and meaning of spiritual experience, and then lays out the actual day-to-day practice itself so that a reader will know exactly what they are getting into and why. This is so useful.

I have a statue of the seated Buddha on my altar. In his left hand he holds the fire of the Dharma, as though to say atta dipa, you are the light itself. His right hand is raised, palm out, in the universal gesture of peace, saying don't be afraid. The authors also hold up their hands, palms out, saying to readers, don't be afraid. It's okay. There is no distance between us.

– Terrance Keenan, Zen Monk, Artist and Writer and the author of *Zen Encounters with Loneliness*.

Satya and Kaspa's living of their Buddhist faith has been an inspiration and a support to me for many years. *Just As You Are* reminds me of why: it offers a beautiful and accessible meditation on the 'Other Power' understanding of our human nature that guides and illuminates their work. What does fulfilling this nature really ask of us? *Just As You Are* offers a grounded touchstone to living out our own stumbling replies to this question, one that centralises kindness, honesty and humour.

– Mat Osmond, Writer and Arts Lecturer.

Just As You Are
Buddhism for Foolish Beings
Second Edition

Just As You Are: Buddhism for Foolish Beings
Second Edition
ISBN 978-0-9931317-8-3

1st edition published by Woodsmoke Press 2015
2nd edition published by Woodsmoke Press 2023
Copyright rests with the authors of the various chapters contained within: Kaspa
Thompson and Satya Robyn

Cover: Photo by Sanghamitra Thompson

Bright Earth Buddhist Temple
34 Worcester Road
Malvern
WR14 4AA

Table of Contents

Love. Of all things least illusory.
Franz Wright

All things are to be loved and revered. Everything shines
forth with a light of its own.
Kiyozawa Manshi

Acknowledgements

All of the wisdom found in this book was gifted to us. We received it from our teachers, colleagues and students in the world of Buddhism; from our friends, family and workmates; from countless books and study groups; from animals and the natural world.

We are especially grateful to our colleague ministers, trainees, templemates and community members at Bright Earth.

It would be impossible to name all the teachers we have learnt from over the years but they include Rev. Gyomay Kubose, Rev. Taitetsu Unno, Caroline Brazier, Terrance Keenan, Shinran and Honen, Zenju Earthlyn Manuel, John Paraskevopoulos, David Brazier, Hōun Jiyu-Kennett, Shunryu Suzuki Roshi, Rev. Koyo Kubose, Rev. Sujatin, Rev. Dainin Katagiri Roshi, Rev. Koshin Schomberg, Nobuo Haneda, Jeff Wilson, Kiyozawa Manshi and countless others.

We are grateful to the Amida Trust who have trusted us to run the Bright Earth Buddhist Temple on their behalf for nine years.

Kaspa wants to thank Mikey for their continued support and friendship.

Satya is grateful to Utpaladhi, Laura, Terry, Mark, and her Amazing Readers peer group.

Gratitude to our proofreaders – Frankie Meitou Carboni, Maria Trotter, Wendy Hall, Fi Curnow, Mat Osmond, Ian McPherson, Philip Wallbridge and Chris Earle-Storey (and we take full responsibility for any pesky mistakes that did slip through). Gratitude to all those who provided testimonials.

We bow to all of our ancestors including our families and chosen families, all the Buddhist ancestors, all teachers of all spiritual traditions, and our great ancestor, the Earth.

All errors in this book are ours.

Introduction to the second edition

It is now nine years since we founded a Buddhist temple in Great Malvern, the UK, and since we originally wrote this book in 2015 there has been much change.

The world has experienced a pandemic, political turmoil, natural disasters and vicious wars. We are in the midst of a deepening climate crisis, which is already causing untold suffering to people across the globe, and the ideological and political systems that caused the crisis are ploughing on with their everyday business of extraction, oppression and exploitation.

There has been dramatic change at the temple too. Three years ago we left our old Buddhist group, the Amida Order, to become the Bright Earth Buddhist Order. This led to a long process of grieving and a re-examining of everything we had learnt during our time with the Amida Order.

Over the past few years we have developed new, more democratic ways of organising our group, and we have incorporated new philosophies and new practices into our spiritual foundations. This process of reflection continues and, although things have settled down after an initial period of upheaval, we hope that Bright Earth will continue to grow and change as long as it exists.

We see Bright Earth Buddhism as including three important elements:

We encourage **engaged** Buddhism, especially in the face of the multiple crises the world is facing.

We are interested in **ecological** Buddhism; a Buddhism that is rooted in the Earth, that appreciates interconnectedness, and that respects the wisdom of indigenous communities.

We also practise **everyday** Buddhism, bringing the insights and spirit of Buddhism into our ordinary lives.

We now run a longer study programme based on our new book groups, and we have a ministry training programme with (at the time of writing) five trainees. Through studying at Bright Dawn, a Buddhist organisation founded by Rev. Gyomay Kubose, we also incorporate Dharma Glimpses into our Buddhist practice sessions. These are short pieces of writing describing a moment of inspiration from our everyday lives, and they mean that all of our Sangha members, however long they have practised with us, can share the wisdom of their own experience with the rest of the group.

There are lots of differences in the way that we practise and think about things now, and in many ways we are still the same as we were. We still acknowledge the limited and fallible nature of human beings, and we encourage our Sangha to connect with the wisdom of the buddhas and the wisdom inside themselves. We still aim to make everyone feel warmly welcome. We still study traditional Buddhist concepts such as the precepts and the four noble truths. We are still inspired by teachings from many different Buddhist and other spiritual traditions, and we are still especially inspired by Pure Land Buddhist teachings.

In this second edition of *Just As You Are*, there are new chapters on Shinran, Amida and a history of Pure Land Buddhism as well as new topics such as activism and outside practice. We have taken out a couple of chapters that no longer felt relevant. The chapter on bombu nature has been completely rewritten. Some of the remaining chapters have been lightly edited whilst others have been more extensively revised to reflect our current thinking.

It is more important than ever to put the Dharma into action. We hope that Bright Earth Buddhism is an accessible, realistic presentation of precious ancient wisdom. We hope that this book will help you to find your own relationship with Buddhism, especially Pure Land Buddhism, and that Buddhism will transform you as it has transformed us.

Introduction to the first edition

Kaspa and Satya

The idea for this book first arose when we were asked by a student to recommend a book to introduce our style of Pure Land Buddhism.

We thought that there might be a place for an accessible introduction aimed at someone who attends one of our practice sessions for the first time, someone who wants to deepen their knowledge of Pure Land faith and practice, or someone who is curious about why we have been inspired to dedicate our lives to being Buddhist ministers in this beautiful temple in Great Malvern.

This book isn't a comprehensive introduction to the many forms of Pure Land Buddhism found in Japan and around the world. It isn't a scholarly tome – and although we have both found that studying the sutras and drawing on the experiences of many spiritual teachers helps us on our own spiritual paths, we don't see it as essential. This book isn't an attempt to convert anyone to our particular form of Buddhism. Our aim instead is to support people on their own spiritual journeys, wherever that may lead them. Pure Land Buddhism works for us but it won't work for everyone. Take what you like and leave the rest.

This book is written from our own personal experience of spirituality and of Buddhism. We don't expect that all Buddhists will agree with what we've written. We don't always agree with each other! We feel that each of us needs to develop our own relationship with spirituality, testing what we are told against our own experiences, and listening carefully to those who are ahead of us on the path.

We are wondering about you, dear reader. Maybe you already have a long history of practice as a Buddhist or in another spiritual tradition. Maybe you see yourself as a spiritual person or a seeker, or maybe you're more agnostic or atheist. Maybe you want to find out more about Pure Land Buddhism, or maybe you have a burning question which you'll be carrying through this book with you. Maybe you're seeking comfort, or maybe you simply want to read some stories about our lives here in the temple with our pets and our vegetable patch. Whatever it is that brings you here – welcome. We are glad that you are here.

If through reading this book you are inspired by Amitabha Buddha, the Buddha that Pure Land Buddhists have a special relationship with, you may want to do more exploration by following the pointers at the back of this book. Maybe you'll find one or two Buddhist practices that suit you and that you can incorporate into your current practice. Maybe you'll find a different perspective on a problem or an existential dilemma.

Whoever you are and wherever you are, we hope that this book will support you on your spiritual path, whether you've been travelling it for many years, or if you're just considering a first step into the unknown. We have been graced with energy, courage, direction, joy and comfort from our travels with Amitabha Buddha. We hope you might find some gifts of your own here – whatever it is you most need. There is a very deep love soaked into these words. It didn't come from us – we're just passing it on.

A note on pronouns

We see Amida Buddha and other buddhas as existing beyond gender, and so in this book we use different pronouns for them interchangeably, including they/them.

Satya uses she/her pronouns. Kaspa is non-binary and uses they/them.

A first taste of Pure Land Buddhism

Satya

What is Pure Land Buddhism? This is a bit like asking 'What is a garden?' or 'What does love feel like?' If you ask a hundred different Pure Land Buddhists, you will get a hundred different answers. This is because they will tell you what Pure Land Buddhism is to them – emphasising the bits they find valuable or meaningful, or the parts that have been drummed into them by their Buddhist teacher, and skipping over the bits that don't resonate with them or that they don't understand. They might describe it in liturgical, metaphysical, or historical terms, depending on the way they prefer to make sense of the world. Of course, Kaspa and I will do the same – which is why we also wanted to include some stories from our group so you can hear a broader range of voices than just the two of us.

With all that in mind, here is my answer. Pure Land Buddhism is a particular form of Mahayana Buddhism. It was formalised as a separate school in 12th century Japan by the great teacher Honen, and developed and spread by his most famous student Shinran and others. Its roots go back to the time of Shakyamuni Buddha, who founded Buddhism two and a half thousand years ago.

Pure Land Buddhism suggests that we human beings are hemmed in by our self-protective egos, and it promises us freedom through the wisdom and compassion of Amitabha Buddha. It offers us a very simple practice – the nembutsu – which can be seen as something we do through our own effort, but is most often described as something we receive through the Buddha's power. In other words, Pure Land

1

Buddhism is honest about our limitations, and it offers us a paradigm within which our foolishness can be transformed into grace. Pure Land Buddhism offers us safe refuge in a world that is shot through with suffering, and it helps us to become more loving and less afraid.

I didn't know any of this when I attended my first Pure Land Buddhist service. I was attending a residential Buddhist psychotherapy training at The Buddhist House in Narborough, run by Caroline and David Brazier. During our nine day course blocks we were told that we were welcome to join the resident Buddhist community for their morning or evening Buddhist services.

I did join them a few times, not quite knowing why – maybe I was driven by curiosity, or a romantic notion about what it would be like to 'be a Buddhist'. I didn't know what to do and so I sat on the floor next to Hussam and Helen, who I'd just met on the therapy training course, and copied them. We chanted strange chants, we walked slowly round and round the shrine room, we sang odd hymns and – strangest of all – we did prostrations, bowing right down onto the floor. Once we did something called the 'thousand nembutsu' where everyone chanted 'Namo Amida Bu' fast, over and over again. It transformed the shrine room into a space swarming with bees, and the buzzing surrounded me as I made a small self-conscious noise of my own. How did I feel about any of that? I didn't know.

What I did notice was a difference between the students who attended the services and the students who didn't. It was a quality I'd also picked up strongly in David and Caroline – something like a deep and quiet confidence. They seemed to know something or to get something which I didn't get, and I wanted some of it.

I can remember chatting with Helen and Hussam after breakfast, and hearing them use the word *bombu*. When I asked them what it meant, their description appealed to me immediately: 'foolish beings of wayward passion; – all of us'. They laughed kindly at their own foolishness as they talked and I felt a sense of relief. Was it really okay to be full of greed, hate and delusion? Could I be acceptable just as I am? At that point I didn't really have any sense of what was accepting me, but I still liked the idea of it very much!

This feeling, and a fragment from one of the pieces of text we recited ('...Amida will receive you, and you may fear for nothing, since all is completely assured...') was enough to keep me going back. These were the little hooks that kept me engaged for long enough for some of my scepticism and lack of trust to be worn away.

We are all caught by these little hooks at various points in our lives. Sometimes the hooks are unhelpful – we stay in a relationship for too long because we get a very small taste of something we are starving for, despite being given plenty of evidence that we're not going to get any more. Sometimes the hooks start out as selfish (we might train in a new career because we want to earn more money) and we end up being motivated by compassion instead (we enjoy helping people in our new job more than we thought we would). Are there any little hooks holding you as you read this book?

As I write these words it is 7 a.m., and in an hour I will be going upstairs to the temple shrine room to run our usual Friday morning Buddhist practice. Later we are hoping to create our first veggie patch in the temple garden, and tonight we have our weekly community meal. Tomorrow we're running a retreat day called 'Just As You Are'. I'm grateful that my first little nibble of Pure Land Buddhism was intriguing enough to tempt me back for more. I seem to have developed quite a taste for it.

Kaspa's journey

"What do you want to do with your life?"

Junko looked straight at me. She was genuinely interested.

I wasn't sure how to answer. We had just finished an eight week course in teaching English as a foreign language. Junko was looking forward to returning to Japan and teaching. Was that really what I wanted to do?

I'd had my first taste of Buddhism four years earlier, in 2001. I was twenty years old. I couldn't have told you what Buddhism was back then, or what Buddhists believed. But something in the few small stories I read hooked me straight away. I found some meditation instructions and started practising.

I struggled with my mental health in those days, both throughout the job that I came to hate and throughout the university course that I loved. When I was reading Buddhist teachings, or sitting meditating, I found some measure of peace.

Buddhism worked.

Over the next four years my practice waxed and waned but I kept returning to it. I read books by Dainin Katagiri and Shunryu Suzuki, and slowly my commitment deepened. In a life that was very confusing it was the one thing that made sense.

I read Janwillem van de Wetering's book about living in a Buddhist community in the United States[1]. I read Rev. Jiyu Kennett's account of training in Japanese monasteries[2]. I wanted to deepen my practice, but doing what they had done felt so out of reach to me.

And yet, Buddhism had offered me a gift of peace that nothing else had. I wanted to learn more and I wanted to share that gift with others.

When Junko asked what I wanted to do, I said that I wanted to be a Buddhist teacher.

"Why would anyone want to do that?" she said. What I didn't know at the time was that Buddhism in Japan has about as much relevance for young people as the Church of England does to most young people in the UK.

I pushed the idea to one side and went about trying to make an 'ordinary' life for myself. I kept practising Zen Buddhism, I worked in retail, I directed plays for a community theatre group and sometimes I hung out at a Tibetan Buddhist temple not far from my parents' house.

I didn't know what to make of the rich iconography and devotional practices at the Tibetan centre. I was still in my very rational phase (more on that later in the book). Despite that, over the course of that year my home practice changed.

I bought a small statue of the Buddha and placed it on a small stool. I covered the stool with beautiful cloth. I bought an incense burner. I placed two tea lights either side of the statue.

I stopped meditating facing a blank wall, in the Zen style, and instead I sat in front of the shrine, watching smoke from the incense curl and dissipate.

I loved the atmosphere the shrine created. I dropped so easily into peace when I sat there. I started to do three prostrations in front of the Buddha each morning.

I told myself that this was because three prostrations take less time than twenty minutes of zazen, and that I enjoyed having a lie-in, but it wasn't that. These practices were touching something beyond my own small mind.

In 2006 I started studying Buddhist psychotherapy at The Buddhist House in Narborough and whilst there I was introduced to Pure Land Buddhism. In 2009 I was ordained and given the name Kaspalita and in 2014 Satya and I opened the temple here in Malvern.

I now have a private psychotherapy practice, and I have been an eco-activist. I have sat on various Buddhist committees and groups. I am a spouse, a sibling and a friend. Sometimes I teach Buddhism. I look back to that young person sitting next to Junko in 2005, and say, "You did it."

And yet, becoming a Buddhist teacher has not been the most important thing. It is a useful hat to wear now and again. Wearing that hat can help with passing on the wisdom that Buddhism has given me, although it is not the only way to share it. What has been the most important thing? It has been developing and deepening a trust in something loving and kind that is present for me and present for the whole universe. Pure Land Buddhism speaks the language of that trust very well, and I'm grateful to have found this tradition. I hope this book goes some way towards sharing the gifts it has given me.

Satya's journey

I grew up atheist, and unlike Kaspa 'spiritual teacher' was never on my list of 'things I want to be when I grow up'. And yet, here I am – nine years into running a Buddhist temple. What happened?

There was no dramatic conversion. Instead, a series of experiences gradually turned me around and pointed me in an entirely different direction. I will speak about some of these experiences in this book. A few, like attending a 12 step programme and falling in love with a celibate Buddhist monk (Kaspa!), were pretty powerful. Most of them were less dramatic. I read a few books. I dabbled in meditation. I spent some time with a Buddhist nun who I thought was lovely.

Who am I? I work as a psychotherapist using a model called Internal Family Systems, and I have been privileged to accompany hundreds of clients on their journeys for more than twenty five years. I write – so far I've clocked up ten books, a blizzard of articles and essays, and a successful Substack newsletter called *Going Gently*. I like watching Netflix, eating good vegan cake, and hanging out with my two little dogs. I don't like cleaning the house or capitalism. On good days I am cheerful, reliable, caring and curious. On bad days I work too hard, get sucked into social media, and try to control others and the world.

This is some of the prism I look through when I see Buddhism and everything else. What you read here will be filtered through these 'Satya glasses', however much I try to take a clear view. Feel free to disagree with anything I say!

There are still plenty of aspects of Pure Land Buddhist teachings that I am undecided about or unsure of. I don't really know what will happen when I die, although I have an impossible-to-prove feeling that I will be going somewhere good. I don't know if there is such a thing as rebirth. I don't really know what the Pure Land is. I don't know if buddhas exist at all, or if they are merely figments of my imagination and of wishful thinking.

What I do know is that keeping an open mind about these questions and continuing to practise Buddhism has been a huge help to me. As I have slowly put more of my trust in the Buddha, the teachings and the spiritual community, I have become less afraid. As I become less afraid I have become steadier, happier, and more open to receiving and offering love.

I could never have predicted it, but running a Buddhist temple is a pretty amazing job. I hope that, through reading this book, you will get a fresh perspective on some of your ongoing dilemmas. As my teacher from Bright Dawn, Rev. Koyo Kubose, would have said, I hope that you will become a better student. As a result of your new insights you might end up going to Quaker meetings, or do some activism, or get some therapy, or make a plan to sit and listen to birdsong for ten minutes every day. I don't mind what, as long as it helps you to become a kinder person. Kinder to yourself, kinder to other living things, and kinder to our holy Earth.

When new people arrive on the doorstep of our temple, I particularly enjoy saying 'welcome' and inviting them to step into the shrine room for the first time. I've got the same feeling now. Welcome. Come inside!

Walking meditation in the rain

Satya

During the COVID-19 pandemic we closed the temple to the public, in line with national regulations. We offered our regular Buddhist practice sessions on Zoom instead, but it wasn't quite the same. When we were allowed to meet outside again we started offering practice in the temple garden, so some of us could see each other in the flesh. We gathered around our big Buddha in the garden alcove, and in addition to the usual silence and chanting we walked slowly around the temple garden. When it rained, we wore our raincoats and waterproof trousers. When it was cold we wore mittens and woolly hats.

When the regulations changed and we were allowed to use the shrine room again, we all agreed that we would miss our outside practice. There was something really special about sitting quietly and listening to birdsong, and about feeling the soft kiss of rain on your forehead. We would miss weaving in amongst the bamboo and smelling the roses on our way past. We would miss the dogs as they followed us around, sniffing as they went.

We decided on a new format – that we would begin our Saturday practice with half an hour of walking meditation in the garden before coming inside. It's been three years now and we are still enjoying our garden Buddhist practice, whatever the weather. I often notice something during the walking that inspires my Dharma talk – a tattered pink dahlia or a companionable robin – and I appreciate that we drag an aura of nature with us into the shrine room.

This outside practice has inspired further adventures. We usually have a slow mindful walk through the Malvern Hills as a part of our retreat days, and we also join our local Extinction Rebellion group for a weekly vigil for the Earth on the public steps in the middle of our town. Kaspa and Khema led a longer weekend walk over the hills, and I keep meaning to plan a sunset chant so we can watch the sun disappear as we call the Buddha's name.

Shakyamuni Buddha spent most of his time meditating outside, and the teachings he gave often begin with a short description of where he is – 'in the Banyan Tree Park', 'near the lotus pond', 'In Jeta's Grove', 'in the deer park at Isipatana'. As Western, modern day Buddhists I wonder if we underestimate the impact of the natural world on the Buddha's life and practice. How was it for him to weave between the trees as he decided on a place to sit? How was it for him to meditate in the soundscape and smellscape of the natural world?

My connection with the Buddha is always enriched by nature. Being outside reminds me that I am a very small part of something huge and interconnected. It reminds me of impermanence in a million tiny ways – a dead butterfly, a new green shoot, the clouds sweeping overhead. It fills me with appreciation, humility and awe. I am grateful for this silver lining of the pandemic, which forced us outside. Now we can continue to enjoy walking slowly in the rain.

Introducing Internal Family Systems

Satya

Since we published the first edition of this book, both Kaspa and I have been introduced to a new way of thinking which has transformed the way we see ourselves and other people. This model is called Internal Family Systems (IFS). It was created by family therapist Richard Schwartz, and it posits that as well as actual families we all have families inside of us – different parts of us that have different jobs and that have different relationships with each other, just as our family members do.

Most of us already naturally recognise the multiplicity of our internal world. We do this when we speak about internal conflicts (e.g. I want to ask for what I want, but I don't want to upset the other person) or when we acknowledge having different feelings about something at the same time (e.g. a part of me loves writing, and a part of me hates it).

IFS says that the different parts of us can be divided into two different categories – the younger, often playful parts, who tend to be more vulnerable and so are more susceptible to being wounded, and the parts that do various jobs for us such as organising us or trying to keep us safe.

When our young vulnerable parts are wounded they end up carrying burdens like shame, despair, fury or loneliness – overwhelming feelings from difficult experiences that couldn't be safely processed at the time. When these younger parts are burdened in this way they become known as 'exiles' as they are usually 'locked away' so they don't overwhelm us in the present.

The parts that do jobs for us are collectively known as 'protectors'. They either help us to manage our lives (e.g. planning parts, self-critical parts or vigilant parts) or they help to distract us or comfort us (e.g. TV watching parts or parts that like to eat sugar). They also protect us from the emotion that our exiles are carrying. When this emotion is intense and threatens to break through, our protectors tend to move into extreme positions to try and keep us steady – becoming hyper-critical of us, making us work until we get sick, or sending us into serious addictions.

There is also something inside us that isn't a part. This is known as Self (with a capital 'S)' in the IFS model. We know when Self is present because it has the qualities of curiosity, compassion, calm, courage, creativity, clarity, connectedness and confidence.

I am giving you a super-quick summary of the IFS model because of the pervasive influence of IFS on our work and our lives. We love the premise that all of our parts, no matter how much chaos they cause in our own or other's lives, have good intentions for us. We love the way that IFS is grounded in consent, and requires that we always seek permission from our protective parts before we go looking for wounded, exiled parts in our dark basements. We love how it helps us to make sense of ourselves and of others, and how it facilitates gentle but deeply powerful healing.

We also love the way that IFS easily maps onto Buddhist ideas. The central concept that everybody has a Self (mostly hidden away behind our busy parts like the sun behind clouds, but always there!) is much like the concept of buddha nature. Richard Schwartz also talks about SELF (with all capital letters) as being something outside of us, which we could easily map onto the Buddha or at least the qualities of the Buddha that stream towards us from outside.

When we talk about 'parts of us' in this book, this is what we're referring to. You might want to take a moment to check in with your parts right now. Are you willing to get to know them a little better? Do you have a self-critic, or an over-efficient managing part that drives you to work too hard? Do you have a procrastinator or a scrolling-on-social-media part? Are you aware of a young exiled part that sometimes overwhelms you with feelings of despair, sadness or shame? What voices are the loudest or the most insistent in your head? What kind of things do these parts say to you, or want you to do? What are some of the common arguments between your parts?

If you are interested in learning more about IFS, 'No Bad Parts' by Richard Schwartz and 'Parts Work' by Tom Holmes are great places to start. You and all your parts are welcome as we continue on our journey together through this book.

Dave's story

Dave is a freelance arborist and ecologist and has been living in the Bright Earth temple for nearly three years.

I came to Bright Earth Buddhist Temple purely by chance. I was living in a caravan on the other side of town when circumstances changed and I was looking for a place to live. I knew Kaspa and Satya through the local vegan group, and my partner at the time had been to the temple on a couple of occasions. I didn't know a great deal about Buddhism but started attending practice on Wednesday evenings and Saturday mornings out of curiosity.

I quickly realised that I was in the company of people who thought like me, and also who I could learn from. I think I had been a Buddhist for many years, I just hadn't realised it.

I am extremely grateful that I have been given the opportunity to live here and to learn about Pure Land Buddhism. I feel that I have become a calmer, more level headed person since living here and am better equipped to deal with the everyday stresses and strains of modern life.

I put this down to the atmosphere here of acceptance and loving kindness, also to my own practice of meditating in the garden when I can. I have recently started the book study programme and have just started ministry training as I would like to share the Buddha's teachings with others who might be interested.

Namo Amida Bu.

Buddhism is also a religion

Kaspa

If you are reading this book about Pure Land Buddhism, you are probably at least open to the idea of a devotional Buddhism – a Buddhism that invites appreciation of an other power, or a Buddhism that trusts that we are enlightened by something that exists beyond our small selves.

Maybe you have always intuited a power other than yourself, or maybe it is something you are just beginning to experiment with. In my own life, I moved from having a very strong Christian faith as a child to a completely atheistic world-view before encountering Buddhism.

When we wrote the first edition of *Just As You Are* I still had some embarrassment around my Buddhist faith. I had been very sceptical and anti-faith in my twenties, and traces of that remained despite my very religious Buddhist practice and vocation. For that first edition I wrote this chapter – then called Buddhism is a religion – partly to speak to that embarrassment. In speaking to those parts of myself I over-corrected and insisted on defining Buddhism only as a religion. We often take a strong position when we are covering up some doubt or fear.

Buddhism is practised in many different ways around the world. Mostly it looks the way we expect a religion to look, but in the West a large swathe of it doesn't look like that at all. I'll share some of my own journey from secular Buddhist to religious Buddhist here, and also a little about how Buddhism came to the West and why it aligned itself with secular thinking.

As far as I can remember, the first encounter I had with Buddhism was one lazy afternoon at work around fifteen years ago. I was browsing the internet when I should have been working (sorry boss) and I found a website full of Zen stories. I didn't know it at the time, but this website was a collection of koans: recordings of dialogues between Chinese Buddhist masters and their disciples, or between one master and another, which were thought to embody some aspect of Buddhist teaching. Here is an example:

A Zen master lived the simplest kind of life in a little hut at the foot of a mountain. One evening, while he was away, a thief sneaked into the hut only to find there was nothing in it to steal. The Zen master returned and found him. 'You have come a long way to visit me,' he told the prowler, 'and you should not return empty handed. Please take my clothes as a gift.' The thief was bewildered, but he took the clothes and ran away. The master sat naked, watching the moon. 'Poor fellow,' he mused, 'I wish I could give him this beautiful moon.'[3]

Maybe my discovering those stories was the flowering of a seed sown in a previous life, or maybe it was just pure serendipity. Either way it opened a door into a different world.

There was something about those Zen stories that suggested there was more to life than I was usually aware of. They suggested that it was possible to take things in your stride and to have a sense of peace. They suggested that it was possible to respond to circumstances in a lively, spontaneous and kind manner. The characters in the koans seemed fully alive, and I didn't feel fully alive at all.

I was nineteen, wasting my days reading Wikipedia and other less interesting websites in between occasional bursts of work. I was an avowed atheist and although I felt intellectually secure I was also directionless and rarely happy. The only bright point in my days was the community theatre I was involved in. Taking on the role of someone else allowed me to feel alive: to feel (or admit to feeling) a fuller range of emotions than I allowed myself to experience in my everyday life. But that wasn't enough. Something about those Chinese Buddhist stories showed me the possibility of a different way of being in the world.

They were Zen stories, and so I read a little bit more about Zen. It wasn't a religion, I read, and it was compatible with the scientific ideals I held on to so strongly at that time. You didn't have to believe anything, just sit quietly for twenty minutes a day, watching your breath.

I liked the sound of that. I was lucky. If the first Buddhism I encountered had looked anything like my previous experiences of religion, I may well have avoided the whole thing and missed out on something wonderful.

After meeting those old Chinese Zen masters in those online stories, I began an on-off relationship with Buddhism. About a year later, I remember calling myself a Buddhist for the first time. There was so much I didn't know about Buddhism, but what I had tasted was very good and I was hooked.

In 2006 I found myself at The Buddhist House in Narborough. This was a residential, religious community that also ran training courses in Buddhist Psychotherapy.

During that first week of therapy training I noticed something about the community there. All human communities are flawed, but there was something else here as well. Something of the same spirit of those Zen stories. Something that I had been looking for. There was lots of laughter. Most people seemed more at home in their own skin than I was, and they were happy to have me around.

Two weeks later I moved in and became a Buddhist trainee on the road to ordination.

There was just one problem. I suddenly found myself in one of the most devotional and religious schools of Buddhism in the UK but I still thought of myself as an atheist. I needed to find a way to reconcile these two views so that I could feel settled in the community.

I started to learn more about the form of Buddhism practised in The Buddhist House. It was my first time hearing about bombu nature, and I really liked the concept. I had been exposed to lots of talk about ideals in Buddhism, but not a single Buddhist teacher I met had embodied those ideals completely, and my experience of Christianity as a child had also taught me to be wary of any ideals.

It was a great relief to see the ordinary and fallible nature of human beings, including Buddhists, being talked about so openly.

When I was taught about Amida Buddha, however, a 'being of limitless influence', I struggled to fit the concept into my scientific materialist worldview. I had rejected Christianity years ago partly because of the hypocrisy I encountered, and partly because the more I learnt about science, the less plausible it all seemed. Subscribing to a practice in which I was calling out to a cosmic Buddha seemed like a step away from what was true.

And yet, looking back on it all now, I can see that devotional Buddhism took hold in my heart early on in my journey, even though I refused to see it at the time. My appreciation for other power snuck up on me when I wasn't looking. I couldn't consciously acknowledge anything that didn't fit into my materialistic philosophy, but despite that I kept stepping closer and closer towards devotional practice – from my brief time at a Tibetan centre, to switching my daily practice from meditation to prostrations, and now there was this explicit invitation to chant to Amida Buddha. How could I make sense of it all?

In the beginning I tried to squeeze my lived experience into my materialistic worldview. I knew that Amida came from the Sanskrit word amita, which means measureless or infinite. The word infinity offered me a way in. I knew what it was like to be awed by the infinite universe. Perhaps my nembutsu could be calling out to that infinity. When I was chanting the name of the Buddha, I was putting my small self into relationship with the universe. Something much, much bigger than little me. Something awe inspiring.

I kept listening to the teachings. I was told that Buddhism involves grace. When the Buddha sat under a rose-apple tree as a child and fell into blissful meditation it was not something he contrived using a technique, but something that just happened to him. He himself was clear that happiness of this kind could not be contrived or conjured up. It was a gift.

Years later, when the Buddha sat underneath the Bodhi tree on the night of his enlightenment, celestial beings and gods appeared to witness the events. It was a god that convinced the Buddha to begin his ministry, rather than being satisfied with enjoying the fruits of his spiritual experiences on his own.

Buddhism talks of each living being having many lives, and it talks of realms beyond this material world.

I kept listening to the teachings. The first time I read one of the Perfection of Wisdom sutras I had to put the text down. It began with the Buddha casting a great light across the land and many different beings appearing and gathering around the Buddha and his attendant bodhisattva, Avalokiteshvara. Gods and angels appeared with the Dragon King and his daughters and various other ancient Indian spirits, demons and goodness knows what else along with the usual monks, nuns and laypeople.

It was too much for my atheist mind to take. How could something of value be wrapped up in such obvious make believe?

You would think that, having just had three years of studying drama, I would be used to important truths being contained within less believable stories. I suppose it was something about being asked to take this all on at face value that caused me problems. There wasn't anyone actually asking me to take these celestial events literally, but that was what I was used to in the Christianity of my childhood, and what I had rejected. 'If the value of the text is dependent on these miraculous events being true then I'm not interested,' I thought.

For about a year after I had moved into the Buddhist House as a trainee, I kept trying to explain Buddhism using my secular worldview. I decided that Amida was the infinite universe, and that the teachings on rebirth were metaphors for psychological states. Everything that I didn't like or that challenged my worldview I either took as metaphor for something else, or I wrote it off as apocryphal.

My personal process of trying to make sense of it all paralleled what happens when Buddhism moves into other cultures. It is inevitable, both for us as individuals and for the new cultures Buddhism finds itself in.

When Buddhism moved from northern India into China, there was a 'matching of terms'. There weren't existing words in the Chinese language to express Buddhist concepts, so translators looked for words that were close enough. Or they would make assumptions about what the text was trying to express based on their own existing worldview, and translate it with that understanding, bringing their own biases to the text. They used a lot of Daoist terms and that gave early Chinese Buddhism a particular slant. If Daoism expressed the truth to Chinese mystics, then these Indian mystical texts must be talking about the same thing. It wasn't until a generation or so later that people began taking Buddhism on its own terms.

A similar process happened when Buddhism came from Asia to Europe and North America. At the end of the 1800s when Buddhism was moving west, a large swathe of Buddhism allied itself with Modernism and the burgeoning scientific movement rather than western religions.

At the 1893 World's Fair, Dharmapala, a British educated monk from Ceylon gave a speech describing Buddhism as, 'free from theology, priestcraft, rituals, ceremonies, dogmas, heavens, hells and other theological shibboleths.' David L. McMahan comments that 'even a cursory knowledge of Sinhalese Buddhism on the ground belies Dharmapala's characterization of Buddhism as free from ritual, priests, ceremonies, heavens and hells; yet this sentiment is often repeated by early apologists and its echo continues today.'[4]

Dharmapala felt that Buddhism in Ceylon was under threat from Christian missionaries and, as a defence against Christianity, deliberately chose to side with the scientific movement in the West, which was itself beginning to reject Christian ideas. For Westerners, a spirituality or philosophy which offered liberation without the trappings of religion was very attractive – so much so that many ideas about what Buddhism is are still shaped by that early publicity.

The Buddhism that I first met used these irreligious claims to hook me in, and that suited me just fine. Without that I might not be here today.

A year after I moved into the Buddhist House I was due to ordain as a novice. Before the ceremony I had to go on a one hundred thousand nembutsu retreat. This was five days of continuous chanting in a retreat hut at the bottom of the garden. During that retreat I repeatedly said 'Namo Amida Bu', from the moment I woke up to the moment I went to sleep. Once a day I was visited by my teacher at the time, Dharmavidya, and I would tell him how many nembutsu I had said. I completed about one hundred and twenty thousand recitations in the five days. Of course, it wasn't the counting that was important, but that speaking Amida's name was a continual reminder of the Buddha's presence.

On the afternoon of the fourth day, I was looking at a photograph of an Amida statue and chanting. I was suddenly struck by a new thought. What if there was more to the universe, in the universe, or beyond the universe, than I had been allowing in my conscious thought? This was a crack in my intellectual armour, and something from outside of my ordinary mind had caused that crack. I went into that retreat thinking that nembutsu meant turning my mind to the infinitely vast universe, and I came out of it thinking something different.

At the end of the following day, when I came out of the retreat, the sun was shining more brightly than usual. I felt a deep sense of peace and the whole world was lit up. My heart was open and buoyed. I was pleased to see everyone, even the people I usually tried to avoid.

The Larger Pure Land Sutra says that the light of Amida is without measure and unimpeded. For a short while following the retreat I saw that light shining brightly.

I could have tried to explain that feeling away. Perhaps it was just how it is to come back into the world after five days of isolation. Or perhaps there was a new lightness in me because of some of the psychological work and the letting go that had also happened throughout those five days. Perhaps it was a placebo effect – I thought something should happen, and so something happened.

All those explanations are reductions of the actual experience, and whilst they might have satisfied me with my old materialistic worldview, they would have diminished the meaning of what actually

21

happened. The simplest way of describing what happened is to say that my ordinary mind and my ordinary way of being was interrupted by love.

I confess, I had experienced similar things in the past. At the time of those past experiences I had explained them away, or denied them. This time I allowed the experience to change the way that I thought about the world.

This is what happened to the Buddha when he sat under the rose-apple tree as a child. It's what inspired him to go forth into the world, and it's what he passed on to his disciples.

It wasn't ordinary human love which inspired the Buddha – he would have stayed with his wife and family if it was that – but a sense of universal unconditional love. He recognised that there is a love which does not measure, or ask for anything in return. He recognised that each of us is already lovable, just as we are, and having had this love shone upon him he went on to reflect as much of it as he could back into the world.

On his seventy fifth birthday the Zen master James Ford wrote, ".. as I see it the universe is God. God is the universe. There is no part of the universe that is not divine. But there is a mystery of part and whole."[5]

I can sign up to Ford's view. Maybe if our eyes are clear enough we can see that unconditional love and the divine are the same.

That isn't so different from the conceptual framework that I entered the retreat with, that Amida is the universe. But what changed after my profound experience of meeting the universe/Amida was that the universe was both bigger, more mysterious, and more divine than my atheist mind had allowed for.

This is my religious sense of Buddhism: that it asks us to place our trust in something that cannot be measured, and that does not measure us, and to be moved by it so that we can love as we are loved by the buddhas.

Who or what is Amida Buddha?

Kaspa

When we hear the word Buddha we usually think of the living human, Siddhartha Gautama, who became known as Buddha Shakyamuni, and who was the founder of Buddhism roughly two and a half thousand years ago in the area which is now known as northern India and Nepal.

As well as the word we use when we refer to Shakyamuni, Buddha is a title which means awakened one. What is it that buddhas are awakened to? To the truths of impermanence and suffering, and to the truths of interconnectedness and enlightenment. Buddha Shakyamuni spoke about buddhas that had come before him, and he spoke of buddhas that would come after him. Mahayana Buddhism, the Buddhism of Tibet, China, Vietnam, Korea and Japan, also speaks about many different cosmic buddhas. These are buddhas who do not exist in history but exist as archetypes – as descriptions of the qualities of enlightenment and as the relatable faces of the enlightenment that is bigger than each of us.

One of these cosmic buddhas is called Amitabha (in Sanskrit). Their name means infinite light. Amitabha is the Buddha known for accepting and loving all beings in their uniqueness. In the Larger Pure Land Sutra, Amitabha makes a vow that all beings who bring them to mind will be reborn in their Pure Land. Amitabha's Pure Land is described as a realm of jewelled trees and limpid bathing pools, where the sound of enlightenment floats on the air and where we are all easily brought to enlightenment.

In Japan Amitabha is called Amida, and the practice of bringing Amida to mind – particularly through reciting their name – is called the nembutsu.

What are we to make of all this mythic language? What is the reality that these descriptions are trying to point us towards? Different people make sense of this in different ways.

In my experience, the best way to discover the meaning is to do the practice and come into your own relationship with Amida. I'll also outline some different, sometimes overlapping, ways of understanding Amida Buddha below.

Amida as saviour

We can think of Amida as a personal force for our liberation. There is something like a real being out there who has an immeasurable amount of care for each of us. That Buddha is reaching out to us and through their power we will be brought into the Pure Land.

On the one hand there are ordinary humans – foolish beings of limited power who will never become enlightened by their own efforts. On the other hand there is Amida, a completely enlightened being spilling over with love and compassion and liberating everyone that calls their name.

Some practitioners experience a very deep and personal connection to the Buddha, who may appear to them to offer guidance and solace, much like how Avalokiteshvara appeared in a vision to Shinran and offered advice.

This is a classic dualistic way of seeing ourselves and Amida, and is particularly in line with Honen's teaching of exclusive nembutsu.

Amida as buddha nature

The Tathāgatagarbha Sūtra suggests that we each contain awakened mind but that it is covered up by defilements, "like gold covered up by filth." The Awakening of Faith in Mahayana teaches that the mind is both intrinsically enlightened, containing all of the positive qualities of the Buddha, and is deluded and selfish.

This intrinsic enlightenment is buddha nature. We can think of Amida as this intrinsic undefiled aspect of our own minds. Nembutsu is then a calling from our conditioned mind to our unconditioned mind, or a reminder that our mind already contains unconditional enlightenment.

There are clear parallels here with the concept of 'Self' from Internal Family Systems, which proposes that we all contain a quality known as Self which is characterised by deep compassion.

Amida Inside and Outside

Some practitioners mainly think of Amida as an outside force. If you are someone whose default setting is self-reliance, it can be a great relief and solace to have something loving and supportive to lean on.

Some practitioners mainly think of Amida as inside. If you are usually low on confidence, finding the spark of enlightenment within can be a powerful experience.

There are dangers to each approach. If we only ever see Amida as outside, we can lose sight of our own capacity for loving kindness and compassion. If we only ever see Amida as inside, our faith can waver and fail when the only thing we notice about ourselves is our ordinary human nature.

Some practitioners resolve this by understanding Amida as both inside and outside.

In the same way Richard Schwartz, the founder of IFS, talks about Self within us, and about "the bigger field of Self... which other systems call God, if they don't have to personify God."[6]

Amida as emptiness

We can think of Amida as a symbol for emptiness or boundlessness – that underlying quality of the universe that enlightenment awakens us to. Seeing emptiness is seeing the deep ocean beneath the waves. It is seeing the interconnected nature of all things. It is seeing the boundarylessness of all things, as well as their separateness and uniqueness.

Emptiness is not simply a value neutral way of explaining phenomena. Emptiness is consummate love. When we see the emptiness of all things, we love all things, and we know that at a deep level everything is love. Mountains and rivers are buddhas. Understanding emptiness is seeing the eyes of the Buddha reflecting the whole world.

Seeing Amida as emptiness is understanding that emptiness is reaching out to us. That we are each held by or manifesting from boundlessness and that we are completely supported. The nembutsu reminds us of this.

This is a dualism that collapses into non-dualism. We are ordinary beings held by boundlessness and we are boundlessness itself.

Amida is all buddhas

Each of the different buddhas and bodhisattvas expresses a different aspect of enlightenment: compassion, wisdom, virtue and so on. There's a value in practising with many different buddhas and tuning into these different qualities. It is helpful both to draw those qualities out of ourselves, and to remember that they are each an aspect of the enlightenment that is reaching out towards us.

In our practice we might invite the wisdom of Manjushri, whose sword cuts through ignorance, or the compassion of Kannon who reaches out with her ten thousand hands to help all beings, or the healing power of Medicine Buddha.

We can also see all buddhas as one buddha. Pure Land Buddhists often see all buddhas as manifestations of Amida. Even Shakyamuni Buddha is seen as Amida becoming present in the world to teach us.

The nembutsu then becomes a window into the vastness of enlightenment, into all of its virtues – and draws us into relationship with all buddhas.

Amida as a symbol for our enlightenment

The Larger Pure Land Sutra tells the story of Dharmakara Bodhisattva. It is myth more than history. Like all myths, we can learn something that is true from paying attention to the story.

Dharmakara is a prince. Disillusioned by the suffering he encounters in the world, he sets off to find a spiritual teacher. He meets Lokeshvararaja Buddha and is deeply moved by this teacher's qualities. He describes Lokeshvararaja as glowing like the side of a mountain lit by the first rays of morning sun.

Inspired by this meeting he vows to become a buddha himself, and to create a Pure Land where all who call on his name can be reborn there and then easily progress to complete enlightenment.

He practises Buddhism for many aeons. Perfecting each of the virtues until he becomes enlightened, he becomes Amida Buddha and creates a Pure Land.

Reading the Larger Pure Land Sutra can reveal many truths. One way we can be inspired by this story is to think of Dharmakara as our own impulse towards enlightenment. We are disillusioned by suffering in the world, drawn forwards towards the influence of buddhas, and will eventually and definitely become enlightened ourselves.

Dharmakara's story could be seen as one of self power. He practised for a long time before becoming a buddha. And yet, that practice was sparked and fuelled by his meeting with Lokeshvararaja. The inspiration came from outside, from an other power.

Thinking of Dharmakara as our own longing for enlightenment invites us to pay attention to that longing, to pay attention to what inspires us and to trust in that inspiration. It invites us to keep putting in the work of Buddhist practice, to trust that we will eventually be brought to our enlightenment, and to trust that we will manifest our own Pure Lands.

In this way of thinking, Amida then becomes our own buddha nature. It becomes the quality of enlightenment possessed by all beings – the quality of enlightenment that we wake up to.

Amida as impermanence

In his essay 'What is Amida', Rev. Nobuo Haneda describes Amida as a symbol. What does Amida symbolise? Both Shakyamuni Buddha and the Dharma. 'Dharma' means both the actual words that Shakyamuni spoke in his teachings to bring us to awakening, and what Shakyamuni Buddha woke up to.

What is it that Shakyamuni woke up to? Rev. Haneda says it is both negative and positive impermanence. Negative impermanence is decay, old age and death. These are the things that lead to suffering and Haneda says that the Buddha was humbled by these things. The Buddha experienced a "spiritual death." And then there is a moment of transformation. The Buddha lets go of his attachments and sees the Dharma (impermanence) as a positive force. It is creative, spontaneous and lively. Haneda writes, "He realised that they were the creative elements of the creative world and that he himself was one creative element in the creative world."

If Amida is impermanence, then what is the nembutsu? It is an invitation to become aware of the vast impermanence in the universe; to become humbled by that impermanence, in the way that Shakyamuni Buddha was humbled; to become lively and creative and inspired as we meet the liveliness in the Universe. It is an invitation to grieve when things fall away, to know that this falling away is what allows for growth and change and movement; and to know that we can meet all of this movement with love.

The nembutsu also reminds us that on a deep level this impermanence is also the universe meeting us with love. That we are held and supported and contained by the unfolding of a great pattern.

That we are being invited to wholeheartedly join the dance of life.

As Rev. Gyomay Kubose said, "Amida is Life itself."

Dayamay's story

Dayamay is a member of the Bright Earth Sangha and lives at Bright Earth Buddhist Temple.

I have lived here since the very beginning and I was involved in the birth of the temple in its previous form, as Amida Mandala, and also in its current form. I am an ordained member of the community, and am proud to be an active participant in the comings and goings that constitute temple life.

It has been a complicated journey for me, having trained in ministry and as a monastic for a good few years in the old school – Amida Shu – only to find the goal posts moving when we separated a few years ago. This meant I had to adjust myself, my lifestyle and my career prospects to accommodate a change that held no real certainty for me at the time. I have since claimed my place in the new order of things and am happy with a manageable level of voluntary and paid Dharma work and a more Dharma-aligned vocation.

As is usually the case, external change facilitates internal change and I find myself shifting in line with the new parameters. New professional and personal relationships bring great joy and great challenges. I can feel that the spirit of The Three Jewels (Buddha, Dharma and Sangha) is at the heart of all of this transformation and gently guides us all on our collective and respective journeys towards higher truth and deeper compassion.

I look forward to many more years of practice and religious fulfilment together with all of my colleagues and friends here at Bright Earth Buddhist Temple.

Namo Amida Bu.

A brief history of Pure Land Buddhism

Kaspa

As Rev. Koyo Kubose said, all Buddhism is reformist Buddhism.[7] Pure Land Buddhism is no exception. Each of the people I mention in this chapter made sense of the teachings in their own way, finding what worked for themselves and for the people around them, supported by their deep faith and their spiritual experience.

Buddhist history can easily become a blur of names and dates, but it's important to remember that each of the people in this story had rich, complex lives and that they were all searching for awakening and freedom from suffering.

They built on teachings that had gone before, bringing them together with their own understanding and confirming it all through their experience of practice. They each intuited something vast and compassionate and wise beyond their own small minds, and went on to share that intuition in many different ways.

Although this chapter is only a brief history, I believe there is value in understanding some of the basic stages of Pure Land development and transmission. I hope that this understanding will give you some appreciation for the ancestors of our spiritual tradition, and that it will also give you permission to discover what is alive in the tradition for yourself, in the way that each of these figures have done. In this chapter I'm going to particularly focus on four figures:

Shinran	1173 – 1263
Honen	1133 – 1212
Shandao	613 – 381
Shakyamuni Buddha	5th or 6th century B.C.E.

We'll start in the present, with what is familiar, and work backwards through time, joining up with the Buddhism of ancient India.

The Pure Land Buddhism of Bright Earth is inspired by the teachings of contemporary Jodo Shinshu priests, other contemporary commentators, and by reading the words of historical Pure Land masters like Honen and Shinran.

Contemporary Jodo Shinshu can be both dualistic and non-dualistic and there is something to be learnt from each of these presentations.

Jodo Shinshu Buddhism came west (mainly to the Americas) in the early 19th century with Japanese immigrants. Outside of Japan the oldest Jodo Shinshu temples can be found in Hawaii, and across the west coast of the USA and Canada.

The founder of Jodo Shinshu was Shinran. Shinran, who lived in the late 12th and early 13th centuries, did not create a separate tradition of Buddhism within his own lifetime, but spent many years teaching his followers to have faith in Amida Buddha. While Shinran's teacher Honen had taught his followers to repeatedly say the name of Amida Buddha, to Shinran faith was primary. When Shinran said the name of Amida he was not asking for rebirth in the Pure Land but rather giving thanks for Amida's other power that had already assured his rebirth.

Shinran's descendents and students went on to create various Pure Land movements. Jodo Shinshu flourished through the work of Rennyo, a descendent of Shinran and the 8th head priest of the Hongan-ji Jodo Shinshu temple in the 15th century. Under his guidance Hongan-ji went on to become the most popular sect of Pure Land, until in the 17th century it was separated into two. The then Shogun (military dictator of Japan) Tokugawa Ieyasu worried the sect was too powerful and divided it into Nishi (West) and Higashi (East). Nishi Hongan-ji and Higashi Hongan-ji both continue to this day, and have both spread across the world.

Shinran's teacher was Honen, founder of the first independent Pure Land movement in Japan: Jodo Shu (lit. Pure Land School). Honen was born forty years earlier than Shinran, in 1133.

Towards the end of the 12th century, Honen, a monk from childhood and then in his twenties or thirties, became disillusioned with his own practice. To the eyes of others he was a consummate monk, but in his own view he was far from enlightened. Searching for answers he read some words of Shandao and had a great spiritual transformation. Shandao, a Chinese Pure Land Master from the 7th century, had written, "Only repeat the name of the Buddha with all of your heart."

Reading these words that had been written hundreds of years earlier, Honen understood that nembutsu (reciting the name of Amida) was the only practice one needed and that everything else was secondary. A great faith blossomed in Honen – he spent the rest of his life teaching the practice of exclusive nembutsu, and founded Jodo Shu. Honen's teaching emphasised practice alongside faith, and although he said that even a single recitation of nembutsu was enough to ensure rebirth in the Pure Land, he also encouraged followers to recite Amida's name as much as possible.

In 7th century China, Shandao entered the priesthood as a young man and devoted himself to studying both the Larger Pure Land Sutra and the Vimalakirti Sutra. The Larger Pure Land Sutra tells the story of Dharmakara Bodhisattva. It includes the 48 vows of Dharmakara, of which the 18th declares that, "I will be not enlightened unless any being who calls whole-heartedly upon my name will be reborn into my Pure Land." The sutra goes on to say that Dharmakara was enlightened and became Amida Buddha. Therefore, we understand that anyone who calls on the name of Amida Buddha whole-heartedly will be reborn in their Pure Land.

As a young monk, Shandao had attended a lecture of the Pure Land Master Daocho, and was inspired to become his student so he could spend the rest of his life practising and teaching Pure Land Buddhism.

Exclusive nembutsu was not the practice of Pure Land Buddhism in 7th century China. Rather, Pure Land Buddhists practised a whole range of things from meditation, to visualising the Pure Land, to studying the sutras alongside reciting Amida's name, all with the aim of being reborn in the Pure Land.

Shandao insisted that all beings could see the Pure Land, that keeping the Buddha in mind was a practice of recitation rather than of visualisation, and that it was mainly Amida's power rather than the practitioner's power that carried them to the Pure Land.

Shandao was inspired by The Larger Pure Land Sutra, which describes this land as a place of jewelled trees, limpid bathing pools filled with lotus blossoms and jewelled pavilions. At the centre of the land is Amitabha, enlightening all beings.

The sutra begins with Ananda noticing that Shakyamuni Buddha is looking particularly sublime. He is prompted to ask if Shakyamuni is communing with other Buddhas (that are not physically present). Shakyamuni says yes, and the rest of the sutra goes on to tell the story of Dharmakara, Amitabha and the Pure Land.

It's not clear if these really are the words of Shakyamuni Buddha or not. Some scholars think the Larger Pure Land Sutra was compiled in the 1st or 2nd century, five or six hundred years after Shakyamuni lived. It may be an accurate account of a conversation between Shakyamuni and Ananda, but more likely it as an account based on practices and oral teachings that were circulating at the time. Either way it speaks to important spiritual truths which have resonated throughout history and across the world, and that are at the heart of Pure Land Buddhism: that there is a love beyond our own small minds that is already illuminating each of us, and that all we need to do is trust it.

The founder of Buddhism, Shakyamuni Buddha (who lived in the 5th or 6th century B.C.E.) taught many things – dependent origination, karma, the four noble truths, meditation, ethics and so on. He said that he taught the way of suffering, and the way of the end of suffering. Although the language and imagery of the Pure Land may have come later, I am sure that everything that he taught rests on a foundation of faith in what we today call Amida Buddha.

In Jodo Shinshu temples around the world, they recite a verse called Amida's Golden Chain[8]. It tells us that we are each links in Amida's chain of love that stretches around the world. I am sure that this chain does not just connect each of us here in the present moment, but that it also stretches back through time, connecting us with all of those who have gone before us, each of us held by Amida's light.

Getting from A to B (atheist to Buddhist)

Satya

Until I was in my late twenties, I was a proud atheist. I took pleasure in feeling superior to people who had religious beliefs of any kind. I thought that they were weak and deluded. If they had to rely on some 'God' to tell them what they should and shouldn't be doing, rather than deciding on moral codes for themselves, I judged them as immature and lacking the capacity to think for themselves.

Whilst growing up I didn't have any positive role models of people who lived spiritual lives. I wasn't given any positive messages about religion. I enjoyed the sport of debates with my Religious Education teacher, but some of her Christian beliefs seemed ridiculous to me. As far as I could see, religion caused most of the wars in the world. I went to a private school and I remember how betrayed I felt when I saw my favourite teacher, Mrs. Rogers, going up to take communion in church. I had thought that she was independent, intelligent and cool. What was she doing? At University, a Christian friend told me that my sweet atheist grandmother would definitely go to hell.

I clung onto these experiences of religion and they propped up my cherished beliefs. We were better off on our own, without leaning on anything. There wasn't anything there to lean on anyway – anyone who thought so was clearly deluded. It took a crisis to challenge my anti-religious anti-spiritual stance.

Anyone who has been close to an addict (or close to anyone who is in deep denial about any aspect of their behaviour) will know that it can drive you crazy. I had been struggling for many years in my relationship with my alcoholic partner, and it was very slowly dawning on me that all my efforts to change him were completely failing. Things were falling apart. I was terrified that he would die, or that I would kill myself in the process of 'saving' him. In desperation, I joined a 12 step programme called Al-Anon which promised help.

The 'hooks' that kept me attending this group were similar to the hooks that I experienced when encountering Pure Land Buddhism at the Buddhist House. The people in this group had something that I wanted. They were a mixed bunch, as all groups are, but amongst them were several 'old-timers' who seemed happy, grounded and wise. I wasn't any of those things, and I thought that if I stuck around I might get some of what they had.

It's just as well that I didn't know anything about the philosophy of the group before I joined as I never would have walked through the door. All 12 step groups are based on the model and philosophy developed by Alcoholics Anonymous and they describe themselves as 'spiritual programmes'. I found the first of the 12 steps painful but just about doable: 'We admitted we were powerless over alcohol [or whatever else it is we're addicted to, in my case trying to control another human being] — and that our lives had become unmanageable.' In other words, 'I give up!' The second step, however, introduces us to what is known in the programme as a Higher Power. It says: 'Came to believe that a Power greater than ourselves could restore us to sanity.'

What was this Power greater than myself? It sounded suspiciously like God. I did some reading and discovered that Alcoholics Anonymous was indeed started by Christians who found recovery from their advanced alcoholism only when they gave up trying to control their addiction and completely handed their lives over to God. This is in fact the third step: 'Made a decision to turn our will and our lives over to the care of God as we understood God'. This made absolutely no sense to me – I had no reference points, and so it was like hearing someone speak in a foreign language. Luckily I was given explicit permission by the group early on to 'take what I liked and leave the rest', and so I just put all the 'God stuff' to one side and continued to learn by reading the literature and listening to people in the group.

Various group members would mention their Higher Powers when they shared in the group, which I found very uncomfortable. However, over time, I noticed that the people using the phrase the most were the people I most admired and most wanted to emulate. I found myself a sponsor (a bit like a mentor) who helped me to work through the Steps, and she told me she'd also been allergic to the word God when she first joined the programme. As she kept attending the group she'd found herself able to develop a unique relationship with her own Higher Power. As this happened she became less defensive when people used the word 'God', and as a result she started to find fresh wisdom in books that she'd previously overlooked.

I was still suffering a great deal, and so I thought that I might as well experiment with my own relationship with a Higher Power, regardless of whether there was such a thing or not. I called mine Bob. I started talking to him before I went to sleep, and asking him for help. It felt utterly ridiculous and even now I feel silly and a bit vulnerable sharing this with you. Regardless – it worked. I started to feel less dependent on my relationship with my partner, less hopeless about the future, and less alone.

My relationship with a Higher Power didn't go much further at this point, but it was my first experience of beginning to trust something other than myself – maybe for the first time since childhood. I very slowly leant into the reliability of the group and the programme (including my very cautious and sceptical relationship with a Higher Power) and I found myself held.

My time in a 12 step programme ripened me to a point where I was ready to let new experience in. When I attended the Buddhist Psychotherapy training at the Buddhist House in Narborough, my time in the programme helped me to keep an open mind during the Buddhist practice. It softened my defences and, as I opened my heart, I began to take refuge and to receive the blessings of the buddhas.

What gratitude I have now towards my ex-partner, who has since sadly died from his alcoholism. He was the person who gave me a reason to attend a 12 step group. He showed me that I needed help, and he gave me the nudge (or shove!) I needed to get honest about my own dysfunction. If it wasn't for him, I wouldn't be here now. What gratitude I feel towards the people in that first 12 step group, and all the books I have read, and all the conversations I have had, and everything that has conspired to bring me to the place I am now. I am now a person who puts spiritual principles at the heart of everything I do. Thank God!

Why do you keep saying Namo Amida Bu?

Satya

When I first stayed at The Buddhist House where I did my psychotherapy training, the students who attended the Buddhist practice kept saying a strange phrase: 'Namo Amida Bu'.

I heard it many times before I asked what it meant. People seemed to say it when they met each other in the hallway and when they said goodbye. They said it when they meant, 'Well, what can we do about it – that's life eh?' and when they dropped a biscuit on the carpet. They also chanted it during Buddhist practice.

'Namo Amida Bu', also known as the nembutsu, is a way of connecting to or expressing our gratitude to Amida Buddha, the Buddha of Infinite Light. Whenever we say the nembutsu, we are bringing ourselves into relationship with this Buddha, or recognising the relationship that is already there.

If we say the name of our best friend we immediately conjure something of them – their kindness, their cheeky sense of humour, their calm presence. It is the same when saying the name of Amida Buddha. When we say it, we are bringing them to mind – a being with infinite patience, infinite wisdom and infinite compassion. When we say the name we are spending a little bit of time with this Buddha and allowing their good qualities to rub off on us. We are stepping into their 'field of merit' where we can feel safe and loved just as we are, and which will help us to become more loving in turn. Some Pure Land Buddhists say that it isn't really us making an effort to remember to say the nembutsu, or deciding to say the nembutsu. Instead, when we utter the nembutsu it is evidence of or a by-product of the fact that Amida Buddha is already here.

I have heard many different translations of Namo Amida Bu since becoming a Pure Land Buddhist:

- Total reliance upon the compassion of Amida Buddha
- Fallible me, calling out to the great Amida Buddha
- Homage to the Awakened One of Infinite Light
- I bring to mind Amida Buddha
- Bowing to Amida Buddha

Namo is namas (or namu) in Sanskrit and means 'adoration' or 'salutation'.

'Nem' is from nien in Chinese (smriti in Sanskrit) which means 'to keep in memory'. 'Butsu' is Japanese for Buddha. Thus nembutsu literally means that we keep the Buddha in mind.

Sometimes we do a continuous chanting practice here in the temple where people join us in the shrine room for an hour or many hours at a time. We used to put up big pieces of paper on the wall which said 'Namo Amida Bu', and 'Namo' was translated on these bits of paper as 'little me'. I can identify with being the very small and vulnerable self, calling out. I also like the idea of the nembutsu as both being something we say and something we hear and receive from somewhere else – it is both a call and a response. In the act of saying the nembutsu our call is answered, whether we can feel it or not.

The Anglicised version of the nembutsu in Japanese is usually written as, 'Namu Amida Butsu'. We have shortened 'Butsu' to 'Bu' as, in Japanese, the 'tsu' is a very short sound and doesn't quite stretch into another syllable as it does when we pronounce it in English. This means we can preserve the six-syllable form which fits into many of the chants that are used in Japan.

We get to know the nembutsu through being interested in its meaning, but we get to know it even better by saying it: 'Namo Amida Bu'. What I usually say to people when they come to Buddhist practice for the first time is: 'Just copy everyone else, join in, and come back a few times before you make up your mind about whether it's for you or not.'

It isn't so much the form that starts to sink into you, but something of the spirit of Amida (with the flavour of our particular Bright Earth approach). When you taste an unusual food for the first time, it can be hard to know if you like it or not. Saying the nembutsu or connecting with Amida Buddha might change your life, and it might not. Read on, welcome any sceptical parts or feelings of relief that come up as you go, and maybe you'll even begin to hear the Universe calling back...

Chris's story

Chris is a full-time carer for her husband and a retired HR administrator. She lives in Northumberland and has been a remote member of the Bright Earth community for a number of years, attending practice and events by Zoom.

I have been a Pure Land Buddhist for many years now. I was immediately at home with the idea of my being a foolish being who is completely accepted by the Buddha just as I am, and reciting the nembutsu is a central part of my faith and practice.

Being geographically distant from the Bright Earth temple and community is sometimes difficult as I am unable to join in with some activities I would particularly enjoy, for example helping out in the garden. However, I find the services on Zoom really enjoyable and supportive of my Buddhist faith.

Kaspa and Satya have done an amazing job at the temple. The Bright Earth community has expanded and strengthened over the last few years and is now a thriving Sangha. I do hope to make the journey down to Malvern at some stage in the future when my personal circumstances allow, and join with the Sangha in person.

Honen

Kaspa

No introduction to Pure Land Buddhism would be complete without including Honen Shonin. Honen was a Japanese Buddhist monk who lived in the 12th century, who selected nembutsu as the essential practice, and who founded a new school of Buddhism.

In Honen's Japan, enlightenment was the preserve of just a small group of people. The best that everyone else could hope for was rebirth as one of that small group of people in their next lifetime. Most people thought that rebirth as one of that group was unlikely, and worried about what they thought was their more likely destination after death: hell or one of the animal realms. Even rebirth as an ordinary human may not have been appealing: during Honen's lifetime there were several famines, natural disasters such as a great fire that swept through the capital city in 1177, and plenty of civil unrest.

Who was in that small group of people for whom enlightenment was a possibility? Buddhist monks. The emperor had taken to signing off the lists of ordinands, which meant that to become a monk you had to come from the right sort of family and have the emperor's favour. In the stratified class culture of Japan this excluded another huge swathe of people.

Women were excluded completely. Nuns were told that enlightenment was the preserve of monks, and the best they could hope for was to be reborn as a man in their next lifetime.

Modern Buddhists take these ideas of rebirth after death in different ways. Some take them very seriously and literally, and some take them as attempts to describe some greater process we can't fully know, seeing them only as helpful metaphors for the different states we fall into during one lifetime. In Honen's Japan they would have been understood in a literal way.

This was the world that Honen was born into: feudal, full of uncertainty, and with little chance of salvation. He was born in 1133, and when he was nine years old his father was killed, probably assassinated as part of a political feud. Legend has it that Honen's father's last words were, 'Don't hate the enemy but become a monk and pray for me and for your deliverance.'

Honen went to live and train in an uncle's monastery, and eventually went on to Mount Hiei, the centre of Buddhist learning in Japan.

When Honen was eighteen he withdrew to a bessho, a place devoted to religious practice away from the more worldly life of the temples. There was a lot of corruption within traditional Buddhism at that time – the selection criteria for promoting monks had become relaxed and family connections had become more important than conduct. Some modern scholars take Honen's move as a criticism of the life he had found in the temples, as well as a move towards a deepening religious practice. There were several besshos on Mount Hiei and the one Honen moved to was famous for nembutsu recitation.

At that time, nembutsu practice was understood to be just one of the many ways practitioners could accumulate merit, rather than the other power practice Honen later framed it as.

Honen was seeking the deep peace that his father had instructed him to find, both for himself and for the people he saw suffering around him. The Buddhist practices he was exposed to were all about getting better in order to secure a good rebirth and then, ultimately, enlightenment. The trouble was that when he looked deep into his own heart, despite his reputation as a wise scholar and as a monk who diligently kept the precepts, he could see plenty of greed, hate and delusion. If he saw this in his own heart, he thought, how could ordinary people whose livelihoods and passions drove them to break the precepts hope for salvation?

Perhaps he was disheartened, or perhaps seeing this stirred compassion in him. Either way, legend has it that he read through all of the texts in the library many times looking for something that would guide him to peace.

A few words in an old Chinese commentary on the Contemplation Sutra spoke to him. These few words, by Shandao, were like a door opening for Honen, letting light into a dark room.

Shandao said, 'Simply bear in mind wholeheartedly the name of Amida whether walking, standing, sitting or lying down; whether one has practised a long time or short; never abandon this name from one moment. This act brings rebirth in the Pure Land, it is in accord with Amida Buddha's vow.'

As described in the Larger Pure Land Sutra, Amida Buddha had vowed to bring all beings to the Pure Land regardless of how much merit they had or have; simply call the Buddha's name wholeheartedly and despite your wayward passions, you will be brought into the Pure Land and from there can easily become enlightened.

Honen felt the truth of this deep within his own heart. He felt loved and accepted by Amida Buddha himself and he knew that Amida Buddha would accept and love all beings, and bring them to the Pure Land, if they called out to him with the nembutsu.

This was not a practice of measuring oneself against ideals, and working towards those ideals. It was not a practice of pulling oneself up by one's own bootstraps to enlightenment. It was simply inviting enlightenment (in the form of Amida) to grasp you and lift you into the Pure Land.

Honen looked into his own heart, the heart of a renowned monk, and he saw that it must be enlightenment, or Amida, or nirvana, or the Pure Land – something measureless – that grasped him, and not the other way around. How could it be otherwise when his own heart was full of karmic seeds and stubborn passions? There was something or someone compassionate that could love and accept him just as he was. This was his great liberation.

Honen was humbled by his own experience, and reading Shandao's words allowed him to intuit and to feel deeply the presence of Amida Buddha.

Honen was 43 when this happened. He left Mount Hiei and moved into Kyoto itself, spending the rest of his lifetime teaching nembutsu practice to monks and nuns and to lay people from all different backgrounds, from farmers to samurai warriors and from politicians to geishas.

He established the first Pure Land school of Buddhism, teaching that nembutsu was the only practice you needed to find rebirth in the Pure Land. Other practices were good, he said, but they couldn't guarantee a good rebirth, because we are simply too wayward. Only grace can save us from ourselves.

This is the deep intuition that lies at the heart of Pure Land Buddhism. It is this that is transmitted from teacher to disciple, and it is this that awakens us when we look deeply into our own hearts.

Bombu nature

Kaspa

There is a story in the Lotus Sutra about two friends. One is very wealthy and the other is not. The poor friend goes to a party at the wealthy one's house, becomes very drunk and falls asleep. While they are asleep the wealthy friend sews a jewel into the seam of their sleeping friend's coat.

The next day the poor friend sets out on a long journey and along the way works hard to pay for food and lodging. A while later the two friends meet again and the wealthy one tells their friend, "Why did you work so hard! I sewed that jewel into your coat so you wouldn't need to worry! It's probably still sewn in there right now!"

A few years after I had started meditating and reading about Buddhism, I was gifted with a glimpse of interconnection. It was a joyful vision. It's difficult to put such moments into words but the world seemed particularly vivid, as each object and being was reaching out to me. I was conscious deep in my heart of how all of us living and non-living beings were rising from and falling into emptiness, and then the boundaries between all of us collapsed and I fell into an experience of oneness. It passed, of course, as these things always do, and ordinary consciousness returned.

Later I wandered around town feeling very sorry for all the 'ordinary people' who had not found the jewels sewn into their own coats, and feeling very smug that I had discovered the jewel sewn into mine.

I cringe as I recall that day. How arrogant and self-centred! Something wonderful had happened, and then a self-protective part of me kicked in that used that experience to prop up my ego and put me above others. In doing so, the experience of interconnectedness disappeared. I was alone again, and sowing the seeds for my own future suffering. Nobuo Haneda suggests that an enlightened person bows to all beings (animate and inanimate) as if they are buddhas. How far away from enlightenment I was in that moment!

Pure Land Buddhism teaches that we are all bombu. Bombu is usually translated as foolish, and is sometimes part of the longer phrase, 'foolish beings of wayward passion.' We could also translate it as flawed, fallible, prone to harming others, limited or perhaps simply: human.

The most profound Pure Land teaching is that Amida's universal vow is for beings such as this. However we understand 'Amida' and 'the Pure Land', we come to know that we are completely welcome in their embrace just as we are.

Internal Family Systems teaches us that all of our negative impulses and actions are forms of self-protection. We are wounded creatures, and in order to try and avoid feeling the pain of those wounds we behave in ways which end up causing further harm to ourselves and others.

Why did I tip from that spiritual experience into conceit? I carry pockets of insecurity and unworthiness. There was a moment following the experience of oneness when I very nearly felt completely undeserving of that experience. My conceited, self-protective parts worried (rightly or wrongly) that if they allowed the thought that I was undeserving to surface that I would have spiralled into a dark place of worthlessness. Instead, they inflated my ego.

It's a far from perfect strategy. An inflated ego is likely to lead to experiences of rejection which might well trigger the feelings I was trying to avoid in the first place. But these strategies are not planned or thought out rationally. They happen quickly and out of sight and we are carried along by them, often without noticing them at all.

The teaching of bombu nature invites us to become aware of our self-protective and harmful tendencies. This awareness can signpost us to areas in ourselves that need attention and healing. The healing is always worthwhile, and at the same time we are not going to become flawless beings in this lifetime. I am lucky to have received a good deal of healing both through my spiritual practices and through finding therapeutic support, and those pockets of insecurity and worthlessness are much smaller and fewer. But there will always be something. We continue to be foolish beings.

Satya called me from the bedroom. Roshi, our cat, wasn't very well, she said. I went straight in. He looked sorry for himself, had mucousy eyes and unusually he didn't start purring when I started to stroke his fur. It was late and our regular vet would be closed. We looked up cat colds and flus and decided to keep an eye on the situation.

I slept fitfully, waking up to keep an eye on the cat. He wasn't getting any worse, but he didn't seem to be getting much better either. My dreams were full of visits to the vets and of dying animals.

A week before this, one of our dogs had managed to get into the baking cupboard – the hinges on the cupboard door had been giving way for weeks and had finally given up completely and the door had come off – she ate a small amount of cocoa powder. But she's a small dog, and cocoa powder is highly poisonous to dogs. We rushed her into the out of hours vet where she was made to throw up, and then we brought her home and gave her regular doses of activated charcoal through the night.

She was completely fine, but it could have been very serious. Both animals are completely fine. The next morning Roshi was back to his usual self, meowing at me and purring and without a care in the world.

I was relieved that our animals were both in good health again, and grateful for the energy that had arisen in me when I needed to take care of them. As I reflected on their suffering and my response to their suffering, I also connected in with how many living beings are suffering in the world, and how little I was doing to help them all.

The Metta Sutta invites us to find loving kindness for all beings, the Bodhisattva Vows invite us to liberate all beings, Buddhism encourages compassion without discrimination, and yet in this human body, within this lifetime, loving kindness arises more naturally for some beings than for others. My capacity for compassion is limited.

There are many wholesome activities that I put my energy into, both in my formal roles as a minister here at the temple and as a psychotherapist, and informally in my friendships and so on. There are also times when I choose to sate my own greed, or to push the world away and hide under the duvet, and there are times when I add to the suffering of the world, when I am angry, frustrated or upset.

There are lots of specific examples of causing harm that I could name – some with acutely painful consequences for me and for others – and I'm sure you can find examples in your own life that point to this very real aspect of our human nature.

The teaching on bombu nature encourages us to give attention and awareness to these aspects of ourselves.

Without the loving-kindness of Amida flowing towards me, awareness of my selfishness might lead me to despair, or guilt, or painful self-criticism. With the loving-awareness of the Buddha, paying attention to our bombu nature can lead to softening and healing. As Shinran said, the ice of our blind passions melts and becomes the water of enlightenment.

Regardless of any potential for healing and change, awareness of both our continual foolishness and the presence of the Buddha is a profound awakening in and of itself: selfishness is an inevitable part of our human nature and in that state we are illuminated by Amida's light. Here we are, conceited, neglectful and who knows what else and we are being welcomed into the Pure Land just as we are. Amida Buddha is already holding us in the energy of enlightenment.

Sam's story

Sam is an ex-resident of the Bright Earth Buddhist Temple, who remains connected to the community and visits often to join practice and see friends.

I come from a Christian background originally. I was a Christian until I stopped believing as a teenager. After that, I became interested in Buddhism by reading The Art of Happiness by The Dalai Lama and watching lectures about Buddhism on YouTube. It had some impact on my outlook on life, and then I kind of forgot about it.

My first encounter with Pure Land Buddhism came several years later when I visited Bright Earth temple for a mindful walk. I wasn't looking for a religion. But I was trying to be a "good person" and to live a happy and meaningful life, and I was hoping to find some sort of community that could provide support, without requiring me to swallow their belief system. I suppose you could say that I was looking for a community that would welcome me Just As I Am. As it happened, I was also looking for somewhere to live in Malvern at the time, so after a few visits, I made the decision to move into the temple.

I found the sort of community I was looking for at the temple, albeit not perfectly smoothly. Being so close to the heart of the community, I learnt valuable lessons and built relationships that have changed my life. The community is made of imperfect humans and my experience has been imperfect – and that's okay! The honest recognition of our imperfect human nature is a key part of the wisdom on offer.

I would not say I'm a committed Pure Land Buddhist – life experience has made me reluctant to make any such commitments. But I would say I am extremely grateful for my connection to the temple. This community, along with its philosophy and its practice, works well for me. I know it might not work for everyone, and that's okay too.

The F-word: faith

Satya

Whether we see ourselves as having a spiritual dimension to our lives or not, we all have faith in something. Right now I have faith that pressing the keys on my laptop keyboard will result in words on the screen. I have faith that the floor will continue to hold me up, and that the sun will continue to rise through the morning mist.

I take comfort from the things that I have faith in, or, to put it another way, the things that I take refuge in. Most of us in the modern world take refuge in material goods to some extent: money, possessions and the status they confer upon us. We have faith that if we do what society expects us to do – get married, have children, buy a nice house – that we'll live happily ever after. We think that if we successfully seek and receive praise, status and fame then we'll feel better about ourselves.

I don't know about you, but sometimes I take refuge in these unreliable things as a way of avoiding the feelings I don't like and clinging onto the feelings I do like, and as an antidote to existential and other forms of fear. I am especially fond of taking refuge in behaviours that become ever-so slightly (or ragingly) compulsive. Some of us love the reliable feeling of relaxation when we drink our first glass of wine in the evening, or the endorphin kick of a run. My own favourite compulsions are sweet foods, overwork, and social media addiction. When I feel sad or bad I reach for sugar, regardless of how effectively it staves off the emotion. Sugar has been faithful to me in the past, and now I am faithful to it – expecting relief even when it leaves me feeling dissatisfied and slightly sick. What are your favourite compulsions?

All of these places where I habitually take refuge (especially the ones with a more compulsive quality) are doomed to disappoint me in the end. As most of us know intellectually, money or possessions in themselves don't make us happy. Despite the hope that we will reach a point of 'enough', this never seems to arrive. Research backs this up, tending to suggest that after our basic needs are met, increases in salary no longer lead to increases in happiness. These things are also subject to impermanence – money, status and possessions come and go, sometimes in ways that are completely beyond our control.

One of the things that can help is swapping our most unhealthy refuges for slightly healthier ones. We might swap out-of-control computer gaming for chocolate or yoga, or alcohol for an addiction to the gym. This is a good thing to do. Ultimately, though, none of these places of worldly refuge are reliable. They keep shifting about. Our favourite yoga teacher moves away, or finances become tight and we can no longer afford to go to the gym. We break our favourite mug, relationships change, and people leave us or die. Because of the fundamental unreliability of the world, Buddhism suggests that we place our faith in something that transcends the material world entirely – something that transcends impermanence.

All Buddhists take refuge in what are known as the three jewels – the Buddha, the awakened one; the Dharma, the teachings of awakened ones; and the Sangha, the community of people following the teachings. These places of refuge are unlike the things of the world – they are reliable. Different Buddhists will have different forms of words for taking refuge. This is what we recite during our Buddhist practice here at Bright Earth:

For refuge I go to the Buddha
The one who is awake and full of love
Namo Buddhaya

For refuge I go to the Dharma
All that guides us to wisdom and compassion
Namo Dharmaya

For refuge I go to the Sangha
Those who live in the Buddha's light
Namo Sanghaya

How does this 'taking refuge' work in practice? People will discover their own meaningful relationship with refuge in different ways. To start with we might choose to take refuge in the Sangha, and to trust that we will be held by the group in a way that would be impossible for any individual to do. We might experiment with trusting that the wisdom we need will come from the Sangha, sometimes from the person we least expect. We might try sharing a little more openly with the Sangha – taking it as slowly as we need to – and see how we are received.

We might take refuge in the Dharma by listening to Buddhist teachings and reading Buddhist books. Since Shakyamuni Buddha started teaching around two and a half thousand years ago, a great body of wisdom has accumulated from lots of different teachers in lots of different Buddhist traditions. We might also try to follow the five lay precepts, which offer us guidance on how to live a good life. Here's the form of words we use for our precepts:

With faith in the three jewels
and in light of my human tendencies
I pray that I may become aware
of when I take life
I pray that I may become aware
of when I take what is not freely given
I pray that I may become aware
of when I fall into sexual misconduct
I pray that I may become aware
of when I fall into wrong speech
I pray that I may become aware
of when I become intoxicated

For me, the most powerful way of countering fear is to take refuge in the Buddha. To begin with I did this by copying what others did, especially my old Buddhist teacher. I wanted to be more like him, and so I did what he did – clipping the lavender in the way that he clipped it, or placing my liturgy book carefully on the floor as he did. This is how we learn as children and it is a very powerful way to learn. We copy the people we want to emulate unconsciously and as we perform the same actions as them or say the same things they do, we learn new ways of being. If we are feeling depressed and purposefully move our bodies into a more upright, open position, more positive feelings often eventually follow. In a similar way, as I attended Buddhist practice and moved my body into various positions – sitting upright, bowing – I began to feel some of the same faith in the Buddha that my old teacher felt.

At the beginning of our practice, most of us dip our toes into taking refuge through first trusting in those who have come before us – those experienced practitioners who also learnt how to take refuge through someone who came before them. This person-to-person transmission of the Dharma is a very important part of Buddhism. Deep spiritual experience passes like a benevolent virus from teacher to student, teacher to student, and if we are lucky we come into contact with enough 'infected' people to be blessed with the virus ourselves. Another word for this marvellous virus is faith.

What are the benefits of taking refuge in the three jewels? Since I became a Buddhist and found faith, my life does look different as I now run a Buddhist temple. Despite that, much of my life still looks the same – I still work as a psychotherapist and write as I did before, and I still enjoy simple things like walking and sharing breakfast with friends. I also still struggle with my favourite compulsions.

What has changed is that I am driven by a different engine. My faith lies underneath everything I do now – inspiring me to connect with the Buddha and to become a more loving person, despite my fallibilities. I have firm ground underneath me, which makes it easier to meet life's many challenges head on and to find comfort when I feel overwhelmed. I also think that I take more risks now – I am more likely to speak my truth, regardless of how I guess other people will react, and I am more able to stand up for what I believe in. It is my faith that made it possible for me to engage in nonviolent civil disobedience, and (alongside Kaspa) to launch a training programme for ministers here at the temple.

I hesitate to make these claims about myself, as I don't want to give the impression that having faith has 'fixed me' in any way. I am still bombu, a foolish being of wayward passions. I still make many mistakes, I sometimes act from fear, and I am still sometimes self-centred, jealous and greedy. If anything, since becoming a Buddhist I have felt safe enough to gain an ever-deeper realisation of how full of self-protective selfishness I am. With the crushing weight of our karma, how do any of us manage to do any good at all?

Through the grace of Amida, I do feel that many good things have happened as a direct result of my taking refuge. I am also more likely to withhold judgement in the face of the vast mysteries of the Universe. Maybe things are unfolding as they should. How do I know whether I'm moving in a 'good' direction or not, or what 'good' is? Some of the worst times in my life have turned out to be my greatest gifts. As time goes on and I continue to gather my (unreliable) evidence, I have tended to trust the Universe more rather than less. Awful things still happen – Buddhism doesn't deny that bad things happen to good people for no good reason. The first noble truth reminds us that we cannot escape suffering. I do trust, however, that I am somehow not alone in the Universe, and that there is something that I can turn to for help.

If you like the sound of faith, how might you get more of it? Here are some things that have helped me:

- Try to get 'out of the way'. Begin to become aware of the (appropriate and understandable) defences you have built up over your lifetime, and see what happens when you relax them just a little bit. In the language of Internal Family Systems, we become friendly with our protective parts, especially those in extreme positions. As these parts feel heard and build trust in us, they can relax a little. This makes more space for Self inside (buddha nature) and SELF outside (the Buddha). Even 'unblending' from our powerful parts a teensy bit and making a tiny bit of room for Self can make a big difference.

- Find people who seem full of faith and spend time with them.
- Fake it to make it – do Buddhist practice, make offerings to the Buddha, and ask for help, even if you don't feel that anyone is listening. See what happens.
- Find a personal spiritual practice that suits you, and a Sangha where you feel at home.
- Spend time on your relationship with the Buddha or a Higher Power. Check in with them once a day with some spiritual practice or even a simple bow. Hand things over when they become unmanageable and don't forget to say thank you.
- Keep saying thank you. If you don't know what to say thank you for, look again. Gratitude will open the door to you experiencing refuge.

Having said all this, grace often visits us when we least expect it – we're not in control of it, that's the point! It is beyond us. We say the nembutsu and we trust that the rest will take care of itself.

My faith comes and goes, as it does for most people. On some days I wonder what on earth I am doing, or I feel frightened and alone. That's okay. Like clouds across the sun, I have faith that even when I don't have faith – even when I can't see the light – the Buddha is still there, smiling at me.

Spiritual activism

Satya

Blessed by Amitabha's light
May we care for all living things
and the holy Earth

I was a late-comer to activism. I became vegan fifteen years ago and dabbled a little with helping out at vegan stalls or handing out the odd leaflet, but it wasn't until 2019 that I was propelled into the world of protest. A friend had persuaded me to go along to a local Extinction Rebellion talk, and as I sat through the terrifying facts of climate breakdown I felt the usual numb disconnection. It was only in the sharing section afterwards, when a woman expressed her despair by weeping, that I connected to my own feelings for the first time. This talk initiated a period of intense emotion – climate grief, despair, confusion and rage.

These feelings launched me into further research into the climate and ecological emergency. I learnt more about capitalism and colonialism, and discovered how clever the huge fossil fuel companies have been at protecting their vast profits over the past decades. I saw how governments choose to protect their own interests and the interests of their wealthy friends, and how difficult it is to force change onto these deeply entrenched systems and structures. I learnt about huge societal shifts in history and finally admitted (with some reluctance) that nonviolent civil disobedience could be seen as an appropriate response to our government's criminal neglect. After much research and some soul-searching, I began to take direct action myself.

When I was arrested for the first time I was sitting cross-legged in the middle of a road in London, surrounded by fellow activists. As the policewoman leant over me and started to read me my rights I began to sob. I could hardly believe that I was doing this crazy thing, and that such a drastic action felt necessary. I was also feeling grief for the Earth, and relief that I was finally doing something that felt commensurate with the scale of the ecological crimes being committed across the world. It felt congruent. As they carried me to the police van, the sadness flowed through me and there was nowhere on Earth I would rather have been.

Alongside civil disobedience I have been involved in vigilling for the Earth. There is something powerful about the sight of a dozen meditators on a busy London pavement, holding silence for our planet. I have vigilled on the canal-side path to COP26 in Glasgow, and all through the night outside Parliament. I have sat alongside Christians, Muslims and Jews. I have been a part of our local group, who have sat in the middle of Malvern every Saturday lunchtime for three years. In 2020 I sat in the same spot as our Malvern vigillers for a silent hour every day for a whole year, through torrential rain, baking sun and snow.

My climate activism has taken me on a roller-coaster ride over the past few years. I am painfully aware of how small my contribution is. I am also grateful for the various privileges which have made it possible for me to take the actions I've taken. As a white middle-class woman living in the UK, I have mostly been treated well by the police. Over the past decade 1700 climate activists have been killed around the world. Unlike some activist friends, I haven't risked losing my job or being deported. I also have many colleague activists who have decided to risk or sacrifice their mortgages, careers, relationships or even their freedom. At the time of writing this chapter, forty climate activists are in UK jails.

Many of my fellow activists, including many of those who have spent time in jail, are people of faith like me. They are inspired and supported by their love of God, or the Buddha, or Gaia. My faith has made it possible for me to do things that I was afraid to do. When I sat down alone, heart pounding, on a busy city road for the 'rebellion of one' action, the Buddha was with me. When angry people yelled abuse at me, or when my heart broke as a little girl took the microphone to share her terror of the future, the Buddha has been with me. When I read the latest disappointing news from COP27 (and COP28, and when the next disappointing news arrives from COP29...), the Buddha was and will be with me.

Nonviolent direct action isn't for everyone. I believe that we all have different parts to play in these crazy times. Some of us will educate ourselves so we can share important information with our friends and colleagues. Some of us will funnel our energy into political change or into local community projects. Some of us will focus on supporting oppressed groups or will set an example through personal lifestyle changes. Some of us will be preoccupied with our already-full plates, as parents or carers, or with our own mental or physical suffering, and that's okay too. If we keep listening to the Buddha, taking it gently, and opening our hearts, our path will become clear.

What does our collective future hold? I don't know. I know that many people across the globe are already suffering, and I know that this suffering is doomed to intensify – even if we stopped burning fossil fuels today, the planet's temperature will continue to rise. Will the human race make it? I don't know. I do know that I can continue to appreciate the beauty all around me. I also know that I can continue to take the small compassionate actions that help me to ward off despair, and that (hopefully) ripple some good out into the world. The Buddha is with me.

"Few will have the greatness to bend history itself, but each of us can work to change a small portion of events. It is from numberless diverse acts of courage and belief that human history is shaped. Each time a man stands up for an ideal, or acts to improve the lot of others, or strikes out against injustice, he sends forth a tiny ripple of hope, and crossing each other from a million different centers of energy and daring those ripples build a current which can sweep down the mightiest walls of oppression and resistance." Robert F. Kennedy

Thank you, thank you, thank you

Satya

When I first became a Pure Land Buddhist, and I was still finding my way with what felt like a very strange practice, I met online with my spiritual mentor at the time, Padma. He told me that when we say, 'Namo Amida Bu' we are saying it not as we might say 'please', wanting something that we haven't got. We are saying it as 'thank you', to acknowledge that we are already supported in a myriad of ways.

I liked the sound of this, but at the time I wasn't clear what I might say thank you for. I'd been reciting nembutsu without thinking too hard about it, but I didn't really feel like I'd received anything. I guess I had some kind of fancy enlightenment experience in mind – blissful feelings of an intensity I'd never known, or a sense of profound calm. I was still waiting.

Looking back, I don't think Padma was suggesting that I say thank you for any special spiritual experiences. He was suggesting that I say thank you for everything I already had. The roof over my head, parents who spent years wiping my snotty nose and clothing me and feeding me and loving me, my education, the radiators keeping me warm in my house, the vets for saving my cat Tsuki's life, the sunshine on my face, the delicious sandwich I'd just eaten for lunch, the invention of light bulbs, the encouragement I received from other writers when I was just starting out, the difficult experiences which have taught me something I probably couldn't have learnt any other way and which made me who I am, this computer, this candle....

Right now I am being supported by the ground and kept tethered to my chair by gravity. I am here and I am me because of the chain of my ancestors going back and back into the mists of time, and because of the very specific combination of DNA that was created when my mother's egg was fertilised. I am kept alive by the correct mix of gases – by this breath, going in and out of my body twelve times every minute. When I pause and examine how much I have received and continue to receive in every moment, I am staggered. It is miraculous.

This is the gratitude that my teachers were talking about. It is very easy for most of us to forget about these things most of the time. Instead we are preoccupied by the things we haven't got, or the things we want to push away. My throat is a little sore today. I woke up late and so I'm rushing to get some writing done before my first psychotherapy client arrives. We've run out of my favourite tea bags!

I also wonder if we tend to avoid feeling grateful because gratitude reminds us of something we'd rather not be reminded of – our dependence on so many different conditions, and our total lack of control over many of these conditions. We're not in control of whether the sun shines on us, whether we will be made redundant, whether our children will fall ill, or even whether we will still be alive this evening. Acknowledging our dependence on so many conditions beyond our control might make us feel vulnerable or frightened. Can we trust that our children will get well? Can we trust that we will survive, even if we are made redundant? As our weather changes as a result of the climate emergency, can we even trust the sun?

Of course, awful things do happen. As we will see later, the inevitability of discomfort and suffering is the first of the four noble truths, which the Buddha taught again and again. When you are in the midst of deep grief or pain it might sound insulting or even cruel to suggest that things would improve if you just 'felt more grateful'.

And yet. I have found that even when I'm up to my neck in difficulty, feeling grateful can help me to put things into a broader perspective. I am still breathing. The plants are still offering me oxygen. Just now, a friend brought me a cup of tea. I am not alone, even if I feel like I am. Things are better for me than they were five years ago. Maybe in another five years we might look back on this awful thing as the event that turned our life around – that forced change and that changed everything for the better. Maybe not. Whatever is true, and whichever small things we can find to say thank you for, we can say thank you.

Practising gratitude helps us to feel more content with what we already have. It is an excellent way for us to weaken the power of our greed, hate and delusion (which all spring up from our fear). But what can we do if we're just not feeling it? I know people who didn't have gratitude modelled to them as they were growing up, except receiving instructions on how they ought to be grateful, which isn't the same thing at all. When the people closest to us hold beliefs such as, 'the world is out to get you', or, 'other people always get a better deal', these beliefs sink into our marrow, and they get in the way of gratitude. It can take some time to open up to seeing how much we do receive, and to get better at feeling thankful. Here are some suggestions for how you can experiment with gently strengthening your own gratitude muscles:

1. Start a daily gratitude practice. Buy a beautiful notebook and make a commitment to writing down a list of five things you've received at the end of every day. They can be little or big – finding a lovely quote, a delicious apple, your neighbour smiling at you. If you don't always feel gratitude when you receive the things on your list, don't worry – it will come!

2. Say thank you. When someone gives you something (a cookie, a bit of advice, their time) make sure you take time to pause and taste your appreciation. If you can't appreciate the actual gift (maybe a Christmas jumper?) you can appreciate the intention behind the giving. When you can feel the gratitude, say thank you and mean it.

3. Be curious about what might be getting in the way of gratitude. Is it a tendency to compare yourself with people who are receiving more, which leads to you feeling hard done by? Is it too much busyness? Is it that you feel you don't deserve to receive anything? Be curious about what happens when you write your gratitude list or say thank you. You might want to do

some journaling or speak with a friend to explore your beliefs and feelings.

4. Fake it to make it. It can be helpful to say thank you, even when we don't mean it. Don't do this because you 'should', but because you are interested in what it feels like. In the 12 step programmes they say 'fake it to make it', which means acting as if something is true and trusting that the genuine feeling will catch up with you sooner or later. You can see how this works when you manoeuvre your cheek muscles into the shape of a smile – hold them there for a while and you might start to feel the flicker of a happy feeling.

5. Spend five minutes every day in silence, making a list in your head of all the things that you have received over the past twenty four hours.

One more story, which my old Buddhist teacher told me after he had attended a talk by Ando Sensei, a teacher from Japan. Ando Sensei is a Shin Buddhist (the biggest school of Pure Land Buddhism) and he gave a lecture on Shin Buddhism which was extensive and very detailed. At the end of this very long talk he said that the whole thing could be summarised as, 'Thank you very much!'

Gratitude is at the heart of Pure Land Buddhism, and at the centre of any spiritual practice that helps us to see our place in things and to enjoy the wonderful gifts that we are receiving all the time. Mountains. Muesli. The wisdom of our ancestors. Ladybirds. Aeroplanes. Hand cream. Laughter. We haven't earned them. We don't offer much in return. And yet – here they all are. We can practise accepting these gifts graciously, really enjoying them, and allowing the warm glow of gratitude to radiate from us into the world.

Paul's story

Paul is a teacher working in a Liverpool prison, a Buddhist practitioner and father of three daughters.

Satya and Kaspa, I'm very grateful for your presence and teachings, being my first conscious encounter with Amida Buddha. My journey into Pure Land Buddhism began attending Bright Earth temple virtually from Liverpool and this has seen me recently taking refuge in the Jodo Shinshu tradition. I regularly practice with a Zen Sangha and encounter many occasions when the teachings of all these traditions merge. I will often dip into your book *Just As You Are* for inspiration, because it speaks to *me* directly and cuts through any sectarian divisions. I am always inspired by finding the common ground between different faiths and so I value your inclusive approach to practice. It is wonderful to connect with like-minded souls and may we continue to walk the path together.

The four sights

Kaspa

The story of what compelled the Buddha to leave home is a powerful myth. Myth doesn't necessarily mean untrue, of course, but academics aren't sure if it really happened as it's told in the story, or even if it happened at all. Nonetheless it talks about universal experiences and contains great teachings, and these teachings have resonated down the ages.

This story is about a man called Siddhartha Gautama, who became known as Shakyamuni Buddha, who lived and died in northern India and Nepal 2500 years ago, and who set the wheel of Buddhism turning.

When Siddhartha was born his father, a king, called upon various fortune tellers to predict the life of the infant prince. Three of these soothsayers said the young prince would become a great king or a great sage, but the fourth said that he would become a great spiritual leader. There was a note of sadness in the fourth soothsayer's voice. He had also seen his own future, and had seen that he would die before the boy's enlightenment and miss out on receiving the teachings that others would hear.

The King, Suddhodana, wanted his son to become a king rather than a spiritual teacher, so he surrounded his son with all the pleasures of the royal court, the greatest political and martial teachers, and insulated him from the travails of life. Siddhartha lived in the summer palace in the summer and in the winter palace in the winter. He travelled between them in beautiful carriages, protected from encountering the real world.

Siddhartha's mother had died during childbirth, and I can't help wondering how this affected both the King and Siddhartha himself. It's easy to imagine that this loss, combined with the prediction of that fourth fortune teller, led to overprotection and to an over control of Siddhartha's childhood. And perhaps the loss left Siddhartha extra sensitive to the woes of the world.

By the time the prince was 29 years old, he had a wife and an infant son. Despite that, he was still dissatisfied with life. It's easy to imagine that a life where everything is provided for you might soon feel empty of meaning. Siddhartha decided to venture out of his protected environment and into the world of ordinary people. He took a chariot, and asked his charioteer to take him out of the palace.

Whenever I think of this story, I imagine them heading to a local marketplace. When I imagine wanting to encounter life at its fullest, and when I remember my visits to India, I think of the marketplaces. Commerce was blossoming at the time of Siddhartha's life. Cities were becoming busier as the middle classes were growing. There are no marketplaces mentioned in traditional accounts, but in my imagination this has become the backdrop to the story and contrasts sharply with Siddhartha's palace life.

Wherever it was he actually went, he encountered four different people that changed his life. These are known as the four sights. The first person he saw was an old man. Legend has it that Siddhartha had never encountered an old person before – the king didn't want Siddhartha to worry about ageing and had kept him surrounded by young beautiful people. Siddhartha asked his charioteer what had happened to the man, and the charioteer explained it was simply what happened to all of us: ageing.

They journeyed on and soon encountered a sick person. Siddhartha had the same reaction. Whenever people in the palace had fallen sick they had either been treated quickly and recovered or whisked away. Here was someone who was really ill and the sight shocked the prince. His charioteer explained that everyone gets sick sometimes.

I had met sick people, of course, before I travelled to India for the first time, but the physical suffering of some of the people I saw begging at the side of the road was arresting and reminded me of the intense encounter that Siddhartha had with this sick person.

Next on his journey he saw a dead body. Maybe he saw a funeral procession, carrying the body to the charnel grounds, maybe a body laid out at the charnel grounds, ready for burning, or perhaps just a body at the side of the road. Whichever it was, it brought home a fresh existential truth to Siddhartha: we are all going to die.

Seeing these three things, the old man, the sick person and the dead body, left Siddhartha troubled and thoughtful. How could he find peace in a world full of such suffering?

With this troubled mind, he continued on his journey, and soon Siddhartha saw the fourth sight: a holy man.

The holy man, an ascetic who had devoted himself to the spiritual path, looked at peace in the midst of this chaotic world. He looked untroubled by the suffering around him and unswayed by the busyness of life. There was something about him that inspired Siddhartha – he saw that it was possible to be in a world which includes old age, sickness and death and to have peace in your heart.

As a Pure Land Buddhist I find this moment of inspiration crucial to the story: right at the beginning of the Buddha's spiritual journey it is not through his own calculation that he sets off on his spiritual quest, but through meeting a holy being.

The story illustrates how we move from samsara to nirvana. We meet the troubles of the world and we long to find some way for things to be different. In that moment of despair we can't imagine a way out of suffering. Somehow we need to trust that it is possible to be in the world in a different way. For Siddhartha the idea of salvation or enlightenment didn't just come out of his own meeting with old age, sickness and death, but through meeting someone who had already walked the path. The inspiration for liberation came from the outside.

I encountered my own 'holy man' in those stories about Zen monks that I read online. A friend of mine remembers a Buddhist monk visiting her school when she was young. Some people find it through simply observing the natural world. We all find inspiration in different places.

An encounter with the holy is what gives us faith that rather than being simply bogged down in suffering, a different way of being is possible.

In the course of one lifetime we will meet many instances of sickness, old age and death, and many other things which have the potential to trouble us, to leave us feeling deadened and without hope. We will also meet many things which give us faith – real people, stories about people, the natural world, the experience we have in guided meditations, or spontaneous spiritual experiences.

As Pure Land Buddhists we can think of this as Amida appearing to us in many different ways. Some Buddhists might think of it as many different buddhas reaching out to them. What's important is to be grateful for these moments when they arise, to keep remembering that we have experienced them, and to remember that liberation is possible.

After seeing the holy man, Siddhartha went home with a great deal to think about. That night his father had organised a party with lots of courtesans. They all danced into the night and perhaps being surrounded by beautiful young women distracted Siddhartha from his thoughts. As the party wound down, people began to fall asleep. Siddhartha woke in the early hours of the morning, looked around him and saw the women in various states of disarray. In that moment he saw them for what they really were, not a beautiful fantasy, but people who were also subject to sickness, old age and death. In that moment he remembered the holy man and made the decision to leave the palace and his princely life behind, and to seek a spiritual teacher.

Here is the classic dualism in Buddhism. On the one hand the impermanence that leads to suffering, and on the other enlightenment, Amida or the Pure Land.

The inevitability of suffering: the four noble truths

Satya

Just now I walked along the long corridor to my office in the temple, passing the open doors of the living room and the library. A small dark lump caught my eye on the library carpet. I stepped into the room to get a closer look.

It was the top half of a mouse. Her eyes were open a slit as if she was just sleepy. Her intestines spilled from the truncated corpse and a small dark red organ lay a little distance away.

I cleared up the mess and came into my office to write.

Suffering is all around us. Kaspa and I both follow a vegan diet, and we make sure that our cleaning products and toiletries don't contribute to animal suffering. We feed the birds and donate money to animal charities. Our pets lead very blessed lives, living amongst many people who love to stroke them.

And yet. We kill worms and other small creatures when we dig the soil of our vegetable patch. We have kept the battered leather sofas which came with the house and so we rest on the skins of animals, killed long ago. We bring in packets of meat for our cats. We strike matches which contain gelatin (made by boiling tendons, ligaments and bones) and isinglass (a glue made from the dried swim-bladders of fish).

It is a good thing to try and avoid causing suffering to other beings. It is a good thing to use Buddhist teachings to minimise the suffering we experience ourselves. But if we begin to think that we can escape suffering entirely, then we are mistaken.

It was suffering that inspired Shakyamuni to leave the palace where he was closeted and indulged by his father, the king, and venture out into the world. It was suffering that led him to his first experience of samadhi (a state of peaceful concentration) when he was a young boy, as his sadness at the worms sliced in two during a ploughing festival led him to sit under a rose-apple tree and sink into contemplation.

After he became enlightened underneath the Bodhi tree, the very first teaching the Buddha gave was a teaching about suffering. He repeated it many times over the next thirty five years and it was one of the most fundamental of all his teachings – the four noble truths.

In this chapter I will draw on the understanding of the four noble truths put forward by David Brazier, Stephen Batchelor and Rev. Gyomay Kubose.

The first noble truth is: dukkha, 'suffering exists'. The word dukkha is commonly translated as suffering but it can also be translated as affliction, unsatisfactoriness, irritation or aversion. Dukkha is what happens when we want something we haven't got, when we don't want something we have got, or when we are confused or cut off from experiencing something. Dukkha happens when we encounter impermanence, and it is the physical and mental suffering that arises from birth, illness, old age and death. It is the truncated mouse. Brazier also talks about dukkha as something that warns us we are in 'spiritual danger' – when we are more likely to close down, lose faith, lose our bearings or cease to follow the noble path. Old age, sickness and death may not always be inherently painful, but they are moments that often inspire greedy, hateful or deluded reactions. Rather than 'suffering exists', we could say that 'impermanence exists' and that we often react to this in ways which lead to suffering.

The second noble truth is: samudaya, 'arising'. When we suffer, a reaction to this suffering rises up in us. I see the mouse and I feel repelled, sad, and guilty.

The third noble truth is: nirodha, 'cessation'. It is possible to harness the power of this reaction and use it for the good of all beings. This is like building a bank of earth around a fire so it can be used to cook.

The fourth noble truth is: marga, 'the path'. If we are able to harness the energy of our reactions to suffering in this way and use them for good, we will naturally live a life described by the 'eightfold path' – right view, right thought, right speech, right action, right livelihood, right effort, right mindfulness and right samadhi.

Some interpretations of the four noble truths hold that our aim is to eliminate suffering by cutting our attachment to anything that would lead us to suffering – that if we can root out the feeling of attachment to the mouse, then we won't feel sad when we see it dead.

Instead, Brazier and others maintain that the Buddha called these truths 'noble', and so the Buddha's intention when he taught them wasn't that we try to avoid suffering altogether. It is more that we try to meet inevitable suffering with as much courage as we can.

Of course, some of us are born into more suffering than others. We are all influenced by systemic forces that we have very little or no control over at all. In many ways Shakyamuni Buddha was a person of privilege – a wealthy and physically healthy man who was able to leave his child with his wife and pursue a spiritual life. (Although his wife and child later join his Sangha, this is a part of the Buddha's story that I still feel uncomfortable about...) It's important to remember that we are all subject to different kinds of suffering and different intensities of suffering, and that we shouldn't judge others for not 'facing up to their suffering with nobility'.

With all this in mind, we can pay attention to the Buddha's suggestion – although we can't avoid suffering, we can live a noble life and try to face difficulty head on, avoiding the temptation to cling to the things we desire, push away the things we don't want, or shut ourselves off in denial or ignorance. We can harness the energy that is released through bumping into things and tripping up, and channel it into doing more good.

I'll give you an example. Last week I had a meltdown.

Amanda Palmer tells a story in her book, The Art of Asking. It's about a farmer who is hanging out on his porch. A friend walks up to say hello and hears a terrible yelping and squealing coming from inside the house. He asks his friend what the awful sound is. His friend says, 'Oh, it's my dog – he's sitting on a nail.' The friend says, 'Why doesn't he just get off it?' and the farmer thinks for a while and says 'Doesn't hurt enough yet.'[9]

Our habit patterns can be very deeply entrenched. Most of them were formed when we were very small, and the parts of us involved in enacting these habits think that they are protecting us from something awful – from being abandoned, from being overwhelmed by shame, grief or rage, or even from death. As a result, we human beings can continue doing the things that cause us pain for a very long time.

One of my habit patterns is that I take on too much and I don't ask for help. I soldier on, getting extraordinary amounts done, until I feel exhausted, overwhelmed, alone and broken. As I melted down last week after another period of working too hard, I felt angry at myself for getting myself into that state again. But it also felt a little different. The depth of the dukkha led me to a clarity that I hadn't felt before. I was clearer than ever that I needed to change my approach to my work. I needed to surrender.

I don't think I'm cured. But I did feel enough pain that day to reach out to several people, to put some new processes in place, and to renegotiate some of my responsibilities. I funnelled the dukkha into doing some things that would help me (and others). I finally got up off the nail.

I find the four noble truths helpful in several ways. They reassure me that I'm not doing something wrong if I'm suffering – I'm just having the same experience as the Buddha, and as the rest of the human race. They help me to make sense of the process of forming habits: we experience strong reactions to dukkha and (when we don't successfully channel the energy into a good place) we handle this by pulling something else towards us, running away, or blocking the experience with denial. They show me how an ethical life is a natural consequence of making the noble choice when we experience suffering.

They also connect me to the Buddha. He taught these truths because this discontent is what drives people, and he knew that because he'd been there too. He taught the four noble truths because he wanted to help us. He has helped me.

Beth H's story

Beth H is a District Nurse who lives close to the temple.

I share my life with a wonderfully insightful husband, two quirky dogs who have amazing personalities and a stubborn tabby Bengali cat. I am incredibly lucky to have a quirky son and delightful grandchildren.

As a District Nurse I see the world full of people struggling.

Four years ago I didn't see life like I do now! In fact I didn't want to live! But I did...

I was fortunate enough to be "reborn", to be given the chance to see life in the way that I do now.

Buddhism was the path and Bright Earth Sangha was the nest. Everything around me 'is' the dharma that I need. I can see that NOW.

For me it's important that everyone gets a chance to see this wonderful way of living life. I live each day now and this has transformed my life. The importance of the Sangha and how it works is fundamental to a nurturing and peaceful existence.

I love how my journey has changed and saved my life. I am so grateful.

My journey is further enriched through exploring spiritual awareness with other inspiring Sangha members in book groups, where the diverse richness of people's lives can be shared.

Like many I am not able to be as active within the Sangha as I would like due to many other commitments. However, the nurturing I get from the community enables me to carry my 'faith' around with me to all the people I meet and look after. That is a gift bestowed on me.

I am part of the Sangha and the Sangha is a part of me.

My life is enriched because of this connection.

Thank you.

Shinran

Kaspa

I had travelled almost six thousand miles to be here. I placed my hand on the wooden door and took long slow breaths. I peered through small cracks to try and see inside the dark temple. This was the memorial hall that Shinran had worked in as a young priest, about eight hundred and eighty years ago.

The temple is on Mt. Hiei, which was one of the most powerful centres of Buddhism during the Heian period of Japan.

Our friend Kazuo and I had left Satya at Enryaku-ji – the famous Tendai temple on the mountain – so that we could scramble across icy, snowy paths to find this place.

It was outside the main tourist season, and so the temple was closed. But that didn't matter. I wanted to be in the place that Shinran had been in. I wanted to walk where he had walked.

Shinran is probably the best known Pure Land Buddhist teacher, and he is considered the founder of the largest Pure Land movement in Japan. Whilst he said himself that he was passing on only what he had learnt from his own teacher, Honen, there is a particularly important step that Shinran made that is worth exploring, and which many people think went beyond Honen's teaching.

It was a very special moment to stand in that spot, and to peer in through the closed doors of the temple. It's generally agreed that he worked here supporting continuous nembutsu practice. This was not the nembutsu as taught by Honen, but rather a practice of accumulating merit – fuel for higher rebirths and spiritual insights. Regardless of whether Shinran had actually worked here or not (historians can't be sure) he had studied and practiced in temples on this mountain and I was the latest in a long line of pilgrims who had visited this temple for the same reason as me – to try and get closer to this great teacher. The wooden temple had been rebuilt at least once from the ground up since Shinran's time (wooden temples don't last hundreds of years). Nonetheless, I placed my hand on the door and felt a rush of gratitude welling up inside me.

Like Honen, Shinran entered the priesthood at an early age. Traditional stories have him taking up robes at age eight, after his father or mother died. Modern scholarship suggests that his father didn't die but instead that he entered the religious life along with at least three children, including Shinran, perhaps as a result of falling on hard times due to the political turmoil of that era. We don't really know what happened. There is very little reliable biographical information. Perhaps those traditional accounts were designed to link Shinran's story more closely to Honen's, whose father did die before he entered the priesthood as a child. There are other parallels to their stories. Like Honen, Shinran was said to have a deep understanding of the whole of Buddhism, and like Honen, Shinran experienced a spiritual crisis whilst on Mt. Hiei.

We can't be sure of the exact nature of this crisis, but based on Shinran's own later writing about how foolish the human mind is, and how he once described himself as 'incapable of any practice other than nembutsu', we can imagine that he looked deep into his own mind/heart and saw how far away enlightenment was.

Shinran did not think that traditional Buddhist practices were flawed, merely that he was incapable of making any progress with them. Understanding that, what should he do? According to a letter written by his wife Eshinni, he was given a vision (perhaps in a dream) exhorting him to seek out a Pure Land master. Shinran went to see Honen and became one of his disciples.

Honen's teaching had caused lots of waves in the Buddhist world at the time. It was revolutionary in nature, and took followers away from the traditional centres of power. Honen's teachings were also sometimes taken in the wrong spirit and used to excuse a wilful breaking of the precepts (this was the licenced evil controversy: some monks were saying that as they would definitely go to the Pure Land as a result of saying nembutsu, regardless of whether they kept the precepts or not, then they could break them all over the place).

The conversion of two of the Emperor's ladies-in-waiting to exclusive nembutsu practice was the final straw. Juren and Anrakubo, two of Honen's disciples who had led the conversion, were executed, and Honen and several other disciples – including Shinran – were exiled to different parts of Japan.

Shinran had spent just six years with his teacher, and would never see him again. Shinran was not one of the most prominent of Honen's disciples at that time, which raises the question of why he was exiled when many others weren't. Some scholars believe that Shinran was already married – breaking his monastic precepts – and that this was what prompted his particular punishment. Many monks had "secret" partners (partners that everyone knew about but no one spoke of) but to marry out in the open may have been too challenging to those in power.

Shinran went on to have a family. He taught the nembutsu to ordinary people, and then in his sixties he moved back to Kyoto and spent the rest of his life writing.

His writing shows a deep understanding of his own limitations. He writes with a wry humour that he teaches for 'fame and profit', rather than any altruistic motives. At one point he writes about having doubts about the practice, but he knows that without the nembutsu he was bound for hell anyway, so why not follow Honen's teaching of exclusive nembutsu?

His ordinary life with a family and with its fair share of tragedies, his clear seeing of his own flaws and limitations, his faith in Amida and his beautiful writing have led him to be loved and revered by Pure Land Buddhists throughout history and all over the world.

Shinran's final leap into a complete reliance on the other power of Amida came during a period of illness when he was around sixty years old. During his illness he had been chanting the Larger Pure Land Sutra. He recounted that whenever he closed his eyes the words of the sutra would appear with brilliant clarity, and then he realised that even that practice was unnecessary if he truly had faith in Amida.

Shinran taught that entrusting was enough. He understood that his personal reliance on other practices had come from a lack of faith in the saving grace of Amida and that he should let go of those practices in favour of accepting that nembutsu is a gift from Amida. It is by Amida's great merit that we are liberated.

From that place, reciting nembutsu becomes not a calling out to be saved, as it was more often framed in Honen's teaching, but rather an act of gratitude for the liberation that Amida is continually offering us.

This was Shinran's revelation. Honen planted the seeds and tended the young plant of exclusive nembutsu and Shinran's philosophy is its flowering.

Radical simplicity: the nembutsu

Satya

One of the things I really like about Pure Land Buddhism is that it is radically simple.

We are told that in order to grow in faith and to become more loving, and in order to settle any concerns we have about what will happen to us after we die, all we need to do is one thing: say the name of Amida Buddha.

If we say Amida's name (which is known as saying the nembutsu) Amida will take care of everything else.

Pure Land teachings have been around since Shakyamuni's time, and then Pure Land Buddhism became a flourishing independent sect in Japan in the 12th century.

The practice of nembutsu is inspired by a Buddhist text, The Larger Pure Land Sutra, in which Shakyamuni Buddha described a king from the distant past, Dharmakara. Dharmakara encountered a glorious buddha called Lokeshvararaja, and as a result he was inspired to become a buddha himself. Dharmakara spontaneously uttered a series of vows – promises that he made in order to create a land where all beings could become enlightened – a Pure Land. These vows include what is known by Pure Land Buddhists as the 'Primal Vow' – that he would only become a buddha once everyone who had heard his name, even once, was guaranteed rebirth in his Pure Land.

Different people see the Pure Land in different ways. Some people believe the Pure Land to be somewhere we go after we die, and some see it as the possibility of awakening in this life, right here and now. If you're new to Pure Land Buddhism you might want to simply see it as the 'field of merit' surrounding a buddha. When we are in the presence of a great person who is wise, peaceful and loving, we have the experience of being influenced by their good spirit and we become more wise, peaceful and loving ourselves. We might also feel more secure and safe – the kind of feeling you get in a crisis when someone is there who you know you can rely on. This feeling might not even be as a result of the practical ways in which this person might help, but because of their solidity or their settled faith.

In the Larger Pure Land Sutra, Dharmakara did indeed become a buddha – Amida Buddha, the Buddha of Infinite Light (Amitabha in Sanskrit). As Dharmakara had said that he'd only become a buddha once all his vows had been fulfilled, we can surmise that the 'Primal Vow' must also have been fulfilled. This means that anyone who hears (or says) Amida's name can know for sure that they will be reborn in Amida's Pure Land, regardless of what kind of person they are or what kind of lives they had lived. Amida Buddha is infinitely wise, peaceful and loving, and so their field of merit is unimaginably powerful. You can imagine that if you enter the physical (or metaphysical) space close to them, their Pure Land would both inspire you to become more loving, and also offer you this feeling of settled faith.

As you will read elsewhere, Honen, a Buddhist sage born in Japan in 1133, was inspired by a text by Shandao. Honen selected a single practice from this text as being suitable for ordinary fallible beings such as ourselves: repeating the name of Amida Buddha. We simply say the name of Amida Buddha, and we don't need to worry about anything else.

Shinran, who followed in Honen's footsteps and who founded Jodo Shinshu, the biggest school of Pure Land Buddhism in Japan today, said: 'This is indeed the true teaching which is easy to practice even for ordinary, inferior people.'[10] How does this kind of simplicity work in practice?

In our experience of running the temple, people don't tend to need the story I've told above in order to enjoy or make sense of the practice. They come along, they are welcomed by our community, and they join in with our Buddhist practice. Either something hooks them in and they return (sometimes later that week, sometimes years later!), or it isn't the right time or the right practice for them and they don't come back. The things that hook them in are often the welcome they receive from the person that meets them at the door, or the peace they feel after spending some quiet time in the shrine room, or maybe even the chocolate brownies – all of which are infused with the Buddha's love.

On first impressions it might not seem like our form of Buddhism is simple at all. Our Buddhist practice includes reading the precepts, silent meditation, prostrations, and the celebrant making offerings to the shrine. Our particular Buddhist heritage is long and complex. The culture of the Bright Earth Sangha has a particular flavour which includes connection with the Earth and a commitment to activism, psychotherapeutic awareness (especially using Internal Family Systems), an emphasis on a realistic approach to our limitations and the unique Buddhist history of Kaspa, myself and others in the ministry team. It can take a while to work out what's going on, never mind whether it's the kind of group you'd want to join.

Our Sangha is a relatively diverse bunch within the mostly white, middle-class demographic of our town. We have people from a range of economic and educational backgrounds, and of different ages, genders and sexualities. Some of our group have successful careers and healthy relationships, whilst others have had worse luck with their karma and daily life is a struggle. All have had at least had a glimpse of the message of Pure Land Buddhism – connect with Amida Buddha and you will come to know that you are acceptable, just as you are.

You could say that the spirit of welcome that sometimes infects new Sangha members is also the nembutsu – it is the way we tend to relate to each other when we feel the security of being held by Amida Buddha. As people continue to practise the nembutsu they find themselves being transformed – feeling less afraid, trusting more, and opening their hearts. They come into a closer relationship with Amida

Buddha and the Buddha's good qualities rub off on them. This is the beginning of faith.

Reciting the nembutsu is a simple practice for limited beings. Thank goodness. Limited beings just like me.

Being a bodhisattva

Kaspa

> Innumerable are sentient beings
> we vow to save them all
> Inexhaustible are deluded passions
> we vow to transform them all
> Immeasurable are the Dharma teachings
> we vow to master them all
> Infinite is the Buddha's way
> we vow to fulfil it completely

Bright Earth Buddhist Order supports and champions the bodhisattva ideal. A bodhisattva is a being who puts working for the spiritual benefit of all beings at the centre of their own life. Bodhisattva activity is any action which brings other beings towards liberation.

As well as thinking about our own bodhisattva activity, we can also reflect upon the ideal bodhisattvas, like Quan Shi Yin, who embodies compassion; Manjushri, who can cut through delusion; or Ksitigarbha, who made a vow to keep returning to the hell realms in order to save everybody there. These are enlightened beings who have promised to return to the world lifetime after lifetime until all become enlightened.

The word bodhisattva is Sanskrit – bodhi means awake and sattva means person. In Theravada Buddhism a bodhisattva is a person who is on the way to becoming a buddha, and who has had this path confirmed by a living buddha – they are the exception rather than the norm. In Mahayana Buddhism – including Pure Land Buddhism – a bodhisattva is someone who naturally longs to liberate all beings, and who puts their own entry into Nirvana on hold until all beings are liberated.

Mahayana Buddhism describes a whole host of bodhisattvas who are so close to complete enlightenment that we can almost think of them as buddhas in their own right. For this group of beings, we could just as easily translate bodhisattva as 'awakened person' rather than 'person on their way to awakening'.

Mahayana Buddhism also teaches us that we can join this host. We can make a resolution to both step upon our own path to awakening, and to support the awakening of others.

What is it that bodhisattvas wake up to? There are many different spiritual teachings that the Buddha gave; karma, the four noble truths, and so on, and each time we see the truth of these and put them to work in our own lives we are having an awakening. The most important thing for a Pure Land Buddhist to awaken to is our own foolish nature, and to the presence of Amida. We wake up to this and we are grateful for this.

From this gratitude springs compassion for all other beings, and the desire to bring them to the same kind of awakening. As we experience the joy of faith we long for others to feel this too: we long for others to awaken to the Buddha's love. To the degree that we have this feeling and act upon it, we are bodhisattvas ourselves.

When I first joined Buddhist groups I found it difficult to trust people, and I found it hard to believe that I could be accepted just as I was. The Sangha is not made up of buddhas; there have been times when I have antagonised people and had people be upset with me, and there will be again, but more often than not in the Buddhist world I have felt held and accepted in a genuine way.

The Sangha, at its best, is a reflection of the Buddha, if a little bombu at times. I am sure that I would not have been able to have the successful marriage I do have if I had not first spent four years living intensely within the community at The Buddhist House before meeting Satya.

There have been times in my life when I have been moved to tears by suddenly feeling, in a very deep way, that I am loved by the Buddha. I have had these moments on Buddhist retreats, and I have felt it deeply in front of a shrine to the Virgin Mary in a London Cathedral, so much so that I fell to my knees in front of the shrine. It's unusual for me to forget myself in such a way, but the sense of love and acceptance, and my own gratitude, was overwhelming.

Although the Virgin Mary is not a Buddhist figure, for many people she embodies the bodhisattva spirit and I felt that very keenly in the Cathedral. She embodies the compassionate ideal. When we experience such a deep feeling of love it is natural to want to share this deep experience of being loved and accepted.

We live in a world shot through with suffering, and in response we can become disappointed and defensive. We try to love, and it's not received as we hoped, so we learn to protect ourselves by loving less fully. Or we long to be loved, and when love doesn't come our way in the way that we had hoped for we become guarded. We inhabit cultures which are already full of greed and ill will.

In the midst of these conditions, bodhisattvas transmit love and wisdom. This world is their workplace.

Caring for others is not an easy job; sometimes it is heartbreaking. Having to watch people recreate their suffering over and over again is a difficult thing to see. Despite that, bodhisattva work is the most satisfying of work. Perhaps this is because love longs to be shared, perhaps it is because of how moving it is to see the moments when people let go of their own defences and their faith deepens. Perhaps it is because the more we love, and work for love, the more deeply we feel loved (by each other and the buddhas) in return.

I am thankful for the Buddha's teachings on human nature and karma which help give us some understanding of why we choose to recreate suffering, and for his example in how to live more lovingly alongside that.

The movement from being loved to wanting to love others, or to bring others to the Buddha's love, can be thought of as the inside-out working of the bodhisattva ideal – from the stirring of our heart to action in the world. It is the natural expression of nembutsu in the world.

As well as completely trusting that process, we can also relate to the bodhisattva ideal in an outside-in way: examining our actions and how we are in the world in relation to this ideal, and allowing ourselves to be moved by what we discover.

At first glance it can look like consciously examining our actions is the opposite approach to being moved by love to love others, and yet it takes faith to examine ourselves without falling into shame, and where does that faith come from? It is the gift of the Buddha. Both of these approaches have faith at their foundation. Both of these approaches are important, and I encourage our community to practise each of them.

In our practice sessions we recite the Bodhisattva vows as quoted at the top of this chapter. They are a common English translation of vows created by Zhiyi, the fourth patriarch of Tiantai Buddhism, based on the 'four extensive vows' that appear in some Chinese versions of the Lotus Sutra. These vows are chanted in many Mahayana Buddhist temples across the world.

The essence of these vows is that we make a commitment to liberate all beings, and that we vow to be reborn as many times as it takes in order to do so.

This is a huge aspiration and it sets up a tension between the bodhisattva ideal, the innumerable number of sentient beings, and our bombu nature.

How can we possibly save all beings from egotism? As Buddhist practitioners we live in the space between the ideal and the actual. We set the best intentions that we can, whilst knowing that sometimes those intentions will be infected with selfishness that we are not even aware of. We know that even with the best intentions our actions can be unskilful, and that even skilful actions can be received in all sorts of different ways.

If I only look to the ideal I can end up feeling frustrated. Why are my actions ineffectual? Why do I feel rejected sometimes when I reach out to others? Am I inadequate? If I keep the ideal in mind, but also look deeply into my own human nature, I find myself feeling tender towards the human condition, both in myself and others.

In this way my own liberation arises alongside the liberation of others. Compassion wells up in me, springing from a deep sense of fellow feeling. In these moments true bodhisattva activity is possible. It is not about me being helpful, or being seen in a particular way, or even about being received well by the other. It is more a genuine feeling of wanting the best for all beings, and a tenderness in knowing how hard it is for us to escape our karma.

Awakening rests on faith, but we cannot force faith into people's hearts. Instead we can live from a place of faith ourselves and allow that to affect how we are in the world. Living from faith, from our own experience of the love of the buddhas, will naturally move us to that place of tenderness towards others from which genuine compassion flows.

A personal relationship with Amida

Satya

Before I was a Buddhist I poured scorn on religion of all varieties, especially Christianity, the religion I was most exposed to growing up in the UK. Why were my negative feelings so strong? At the time I had a powerful need to feel in control of my life. I saw any talk of dependency on deities or external moral frameworks as a challenge to this self-sufficiency, and I didn't want to consider that these ideas might have any merit.

I also didn't believe in the existence of the divine – it just didn't make any logical sense to me. Why would people choose to rely on an imaginary spiritual being when they could depend on themselves instead? We can always take refuge in ourselves and in our ability to control everything around us, can't we? As I've said elsewhere, after living with an alcoholic for many years, I discovered that I could not.

After I became a Buddhist, and as the years ticked on, I found myself attracted to a theme in Christian books that I couldn't seem to find in the Buddhist books I was reading. The Christian writers speak of it quite naturally, as if it is something the reader is taking for granted. This theme is the writer's personal relationship with God.

As I read more, I saw that although these personal relationships varied for the individual writers they often had three primary characteristics: a deep feeling of love towards God, a feeling of being loved and looked after in return (and the accompanying feelings of faith, comfort and joy), and a willingness to do whatever God asks them to do. This willingness to act on God's behalf can be seen as an expression of this deep love, and also as an acknowledgement that God knows much more than we do and so can guide us more skilfully than we can guide ourselves.

Saying the nembutsu and engaging in other forms of Buddhist practice helps me get closer to Amida: to deepen my personal relationship with them, to open myself up to their grace and to put my own self-protective ideas aside to make space for something else. As a result, I certainly feel more love and gratitude towards the buddhas; for all they have given me, and for the refuge I find in the Buddha, Dharma and Sangha. I also have the experience (sometimes in a vague hard-to-put-my-finger-on way, sometimes more strongly) of being loved and cared for by the Buddha. But what about the third characteristic? What does it mean to do what God or Buddha wants us to do, rather than what we want to do? How can we tell the difference? Is it always sensible?

Is there a God-like being who has a plan for my life, or who knows more than I do about what I should do next? I don't know. Sometimes this idea seems far-fetched and ridiculous to me. How could there be anything that 'knows better' in such a complex world, and even if there was, why would it bother to look after my destiny as opposed to the destiny of countless other billions of people?

At other times, especially when I stop trying to think about it rationally and just immerse myself in this 'way of being', it seems possible. There are times when it does seem that something-other-than-me knows more than I do. I might hear a stranger say something that profoundly speaks to a dilemma I'm having, or read something in a book and then hear the same thing somewhere else the next day. I might pull a Tarot card and get some wisdom that unlocks a new way forward. I might ask the Buddha a question, and have a sense of an answer coming back (they often seem to say, 'don't worry about it'.)

Maybe these answers are coming from the Earth as Gaia – a giant organism, regulating herself with a series of subtle and complicated manoeuvres. Maybe they emerge somehow from the sum of all of our wisdom. Maybe it's simply the working of my own subconscious, bringing me answers that I can't access when I think of what 'I' should do. Whatever the explanation, I have a strong sense of a grand benign 'unfolding', which is wiser, more complex and more marvellous than the plan my own little brain is able to come up with.

My (sometimes wavering) belief in the benefits of trusting in an unknown-to-me unfolding rather than my own plan has evolved after years of observation and experimentation. To begin with, I watched people who seemed to have a deeply spiritual element to their lives, noticing what seemed to be different about them. They exuded a deep quiet confidence, and (as I would later make the link) this allowed them to take more risks, and to be more courageous in their loving of others. I saw this most clearly when I took part in 12 step groups. Rather than becoming weaker, the people who were more dependent on their Higher Powers seemed to be more 'together' – more whole as people. I began to try this out for myself.

Does 'letting Amida decide' send little shivers of cynical incredulity through you? That's okay – I get that! Our cynical parts are important – they help us to check things out thoroughly and they protect us from being hoodwinked or from unskilfully handing over responsibility to someone or something else. I'll say a little more about how it works for me and if you decide not to experiment with it yourself then I totally understand.

If I am feeling stuck or tangled about something then I make a decision to 'hand it over' to Amida in my mind, trusting that they will work it out. It may be that I need to make a big decision about whether to continue a project, or I might feel overwhelmed by feelings of frustration with someone without really knowing why. This 'handing over' usually gives me some immediate relief for two reasons. The first is that in handing it over I've acknowledged that I'm not handling it very well myself – admitting that I'm not the Master of the Universe after all and that some things are beyond me is always a good thing for me to do. It's actually quite a relief not to be Master of the Universe... The second reason is that once I've handed it over I'm not on my own with it any more – Amida or the Universe is helping me.

If it's a big and gnarly problem, I might have to hand it over again and again as it returns to haunt me in the small hours of the night or as I worry away at it, playing out the same scenarios endlessly. After I've handed it over I will then patiently keep my ears and eyes open for anything that pertains to my problem. Answers might come to me through something I overhear in a shop, or from a thought that arises from nowhere, or from a paragraph I read in a book. It might be that the answer comes more directly, as I sit with the Buddha and have a surprising new insight. Sometimes I even hear something like the voice of the Buddha giving me advice or telling me what to do. This is usually a short phrase rather than specific instructions and is often something like 'there's no need to worry' or 'just wait'.

It's worth saying at this point that the solution to my problem may not come immediately, or in anything like the timescale I had in mind! When I was in a relationship with my alcoholic ex-partner and didn't know whether I should stay or go, I was advised to stay in the relationship, keep looking at my own part in the difficulties, keep handing the dilemma over to my Higher Power and wait. It was a year of waiting (and attending a 12 step programme) before the solution came to me, and when it came it was crystal clear. I hadn't been ready to hear the solution earlier in the year. It would have been much harder to live that year in a state of not knowing, without trusting that there was some kind of bigger plan which I didn't understand just yet. This year of not knowing and working on myself was a year of deep personal change, during which I learnt lessons which have proved crucial to me ever since.

How do we know that the solutions that come to us are 'God's will and not mine'? Throughout history many evil acts have been justified by using God's name ('God told me to do it') – and so this is a serious and important question. Our egos are sneaky and they may try to find ways to disguise our secret desires as a 'message from the Universe'. Here are a few suggestions for checks and balances.

- Amida's solutions will always come from a place of more love and less fear. Will your new solution lead towards love, or away from it? If the latter, then it's not coming from the Buddha!

- If in doubt (or even as a common practice), do check out any guidance you receive from the Buddha with trusted friends and/or Buddhist teachers.
- Guidance from outside might present itself to us persistently; for example, three different people might give us the same advice that is counter to the direction we're currently heading in.
- Sometimes on hearing the solution we might feel a (sometimes reluctant!) knowing in our stomachs that this is what we have to do. It feels somehow *right*.
- The solution may take us further than we would go on our own – a sign that the insights may be from outside our own ego structures. One of my 12 step sponsors would say that God's plan for her was way grander and more magnificent than she could ever have imagined for herself.

From a Buddhist perspective we would say that Dharma (or truth) is seeing things-as-they-are, and that we can only see things-as-they-are if we are looking through eyes unclouded by ego. One way of doing this is with help from outside of ourselves – the Buddha intervenes and whips away the veil from our eyes.

The biggest example of this working in my life is the one I gave earlier in the book about running a temple full of templemates – the last thing I thought I ever wanted to do. Amida knew better! Another characteristic of the solutions that come from Amida is that we can trust that we will only ever be given what we can handle. I love what Jesus said about God: that his yoke is light. This has been my experience.

An important question which arises from this conversation is, is the Buddha an interventionist divine figure? Do the buddhas have the opportunity to make changes to our lives? If we ask for their help with something specific, for example, healing sickness, is it within their power to do so?

This is an old problem for Christianity. How can God have made a 'perfect world' and then allow babies to die at birth? How can it be 'God's will' for my young friend to have a brain tumour? There are various ways of squaring this. My tentative answer, for now, is that the buddhas don't have the power to change things or to stop our suffering. They exist in the same Universe as we do – one shot through with dukkha, randomness, and things that are terribly unfair.

What they can do is accompany us through our difficulties. They can bring us strength and comfort, and help us see the opportunity of learning from our trials. They can remind us of the bigger picture and give us a taste of the truth of impermanence and non-duality which puts everything into a different perspective. They're not saying that our suffering is their 'will', though, or that they'll save us from it if we pray hard enough. Karma has its own life and it rolls on regardless of them or us.

Having said that, who knows?

As a summary, my personal relationship with Amida means that I trust them to know best, that I feel love towards them, and that I feel their love towards me. I don't feel this love as a blanket, cover-all love that Amida feels for everyone, but as a very specific love-towards-Satya, as Amida knows me better than I know myself.

Being loved is my favourite part about being a Buddhist, and the most unexpected. I feel like I'm in a relationship with something that never lets me down, that loves me unconditionally, and that is always there for me. I feel the glow of this love and I know that it exists underneath everything else, supporting me and giving me courage.

What can we do to get closer to our own Higher Power? There are a million different answers to this question as each of us will find our way in our own unique fashion. In fact, rather than thinking about it as finding your way, you might want to think of it as being led, and of allowing yourself to be led.

Look for clues in the Universe. Are you drawn to attend a particular class, read a spiritual book or spend time in a church? Do you want to get to know a spiritual acquaintance better? Are you interested in the idea of having a small shrine in your bedroom, or going for walks in nature and practising gratitude? How might you approach your Higher Power – by saying please (praying) or thank you? By handing your problems over? By putting yourself in her hands, even if you don't know what that means or how you might carry it out? Maybe a phrase jumps out at you when you read a book, or you see a quote from Saint Francis of Assisi on social media. Write it down. Repeat it regularly. See what happens.

Nobody can tell us how (or whether) our relationship with the buddhas will develop and deepen. We wouldn't dream of suggesting to our single friends that they kiss a man we think they'd be suited to, or squeeze them both into a hug when they don't even know each other's names. What we can do is spend time with those people who've journeyed before us and see what rubs off on us. We can put aside any defensiveness or cynicism that arises, just for now, and see it as a playful experiment. We can experiment with trusting Amida, alongside our feelings of resistance.

Letting go into God can be terrifying – we are surrendering everything that we think keeps us safe: our self-sufficiency, our control, our identities, our self-centred empires – but it is also the most delicious thing I have ever tasted. I'd love for you to get a taste of it too.

Katie's story

Katie is an early years manager, wife, mum to three teenagers, daughter, sister & friend.

I came across the Bright Earth temple through the modern way of Google search after reading Russell Brand's book, 'Recovery'. At nearly three years sober, attending the temple has really enabled me to stay on track with sobriety, embracing a positive mindset and meeting others on their own journeys. I adore Saturday morning practice which starts with mindfulness and a silent walk around the temple garden and I am always greeted by two adorable resident dogs with great excitement.

The Bright Earth Buddhist Temple is a warm and welcoming community I feel very proud to be a part of.

Deep listening

Kaspa

I have learnt a great deal from deep listening, both to other people and to Amida.

One of the practices we do here at Bright Earth is a 'listening circle'. We sit in a circle and take turns to speak. We use a stone to signify which person is speaking and being listened to, passing it around the group until each person has been heard.

Back in 2006, when I moved into the Buddhist community in Leicestershire, I was very nervous of meetings like these. We would gather as a household once a week, and sometimes the training community (those of us in the community who were ordained, or on the road to ordination) would meet separately as well.

One evening, after we had finished our Sunday afternoon practice session, after we had eaten dinner, and after the washing up had been done, I went to the bathroom at the top of the house. The bathroom was nestled under the eaves of the house and had a sloped ceiling. As I was there I heard the bell ring downstairs to summon us to the listening circle. I leant my head against the sloped ceiling and took a deep breath. As the bell rang nervousness shot through me. I didn't want to go downstairs.

What was I worried about? I was thinking more about speaking and being heard than I was about the act of listening. I was worried that if I shared honestly and people started to see me for who I really was that they would reject me. I was also worried that I didn't know myself that well either, and perhaps if I started to share honestly I wouldn't like what I heard.

I did go to the meeting. I would like to say that I went out of a sense of it being a good thing to do, but the truth is if I didn't go someone would have asked me why I hadn't, and having to answer by saying that I was nervous would have left me feeling more vulnerable than going to the meeting.

When I did speak people listened, and most of the time they listened without judgement. If there were reactions from people that worried me, they were held in the larger container of the group. No single person embodies complete love and acceptance all of the time, but the whole of the Sangha is greater than the sum of its parts. My experience of the group was that it was accepting and without judgement.

Not only did I begin to feel comfortable in these groups, I also began to look forward to them. When I spoke they gave me an experience of being accepted just as I was, and when I listened I learnt about the conditions of others' lives. The more deeply I understood their lives, the easier it was to love them.

Now I understand that these meetings are holy spaces. The Sangha at its best is a reflection of the Buddha, and coming together in this way can facilitate a deep experience of relationship with the Sangha as a buddha. More often than not there is a great teaching in the words of someone else. It is not unusual that what someone shares from their heart speaks directly to a question I have been holding. Perhaps someone talks about a difficult relationship with a friend, and I learn something about my own friendships, or someone shares about coming to terms with grief, and some of my own grief finds solace.

Looking back on my first experiences of these kinds of groups, I wish I'd understood early on that listening to others is as powerful as being listened to. In those days my nerves came from imagining the moment when I would have to speak, so much so that I wasn't really listening to what others were sharing. If I had been able to give all of my attention to listening, I'm sure I would have felt a lot less nervous.

And of course, the more I was able to be honest about my nerves, the less they got in the way of listening and speaking.

We can listen to each other deeply, we can listen to the Sangha as the voice of the Buddha, and we can listen directly to the Buddha.

We can listen to Amida Buddha as they speak directly to our heart and we can listen to the words of Shakyamuni Buddha through recorded teachings.

There are many texts which record what Buddha Shakyamuni said and taught during his lifetime, and only a few which mention Amida Buddha, but all buddhas act and teach with the same spirit.

There's a great deal of wisdom in the teachings of Shakyamuni: advice on meditations and suggestions on how to live a good life, as well as psychological and spiritual teachings. Through reading and studying these, and the commentaries of later Buddhist teachers, we can get a sense of the character of the buddhas and what they stand for.

If we want the same kind of happiness and freedom the buddhas have then we should get to know them in this way.

Sometimes when we encounter the Buddha in this form, something in the teaching will speak to us directly. It will reach out across time and space and answer a question we have been asking or show us some guidance that we didn't even know we were looking for. If I read a teaching more than once something different might speak to me each time I read the text.

Sometimes when I pray I get an answer. I don't pray for a winning lottery ticket, or any kind of intervention in the material world (although sometimes things happen which feel like grace) but for wisdom and guidance and for faith.

I sit in front of a shrine, I make an offering and I turn my mind to the Buddha. The experience is like tuning in. The dial is usually set to 'Kaspa' and I need to turn it to 'Amida'.

I have done this when I've become stuck in relationships with friends, and I often do this before giving a talk, particularly if I'm nervous.

I trust that this is also a form of nembutsu, but rather than asking for awakening in general, rather than remembering boundlessness, I am asking for specific guidance.

I suppose you might call it a deep intuition, or the best part of my unconscious mind at work, but sometimes the answer that comes back is so far outside of what I know, that I am sure it comes from outside me. The felt sense is like this: the Buddha is here. Sometimes the answer is clear and specific and sometimes I am just reminded of boundlessness and the presence of love.

Occasionally I know what the answer will be before I ask, and in these cases what I am really asking for is faith and courage to do the right thing, or to be accepted even if I cannot do the right thing. Trusting that the Buddha is near assures me that all will be well.

You might ask, how do I know it's the Buddha and not a more wayward spirit? This is where understanding the character of the Buddha is important.

I have met the Buddha not only through feeling their presence in my practice and prayers, but also through Buddhist teachings. I know buddhas act in line with the precepts, so if I am advised to break the precepts, it's probably not a buddha speaking to me.

It's also true that the more I get to know the selfish parts of myself the easier it is to tell the difference between what I want and what the Buddha wants.

I went through a phase of asking for help, and then becoming resentful that what I had asked for help with was still difficult.

During that time, asking, "What can I do for the Buddha?" was a better approach.

When I asked what I could offer, rather than what could I receive, it undermined that resentment.

Instead of asking the Buddha to make life easier for me, I asked for direction to whatever would bring liberation for myself and others. That connects me with a bigger story than the one I was inhabiting, which was about serving my own ends, and it asked me to step up for a bigger cause. Difficulty became something to be met wholeheartedly rather than avoided. My own freedom came from going into the world to perform the Buddha's work.

When I ask what I can offer the Buddha, sometimes I am directed towards work that takes me out of my comfort zone, and sometimes I am directed to work that is restorative. Sometimes the former becomes the latter when it is held in the Buddha's light.

We hide from the truth in order to keep ourselves safe (or at least that's what our ego believes). Deep listening, to each other, ourselves and the Buddha, brings us closer to what is true and to the real safety of liberation.

Safe spaces

Satya

For many years on Sunday evenings we held a listening circle in the temple as Kaspa described above – taking turns at holding a stone so we could speak and be listened to. We now hold them as a part of our occasional retreat days.

These kinds of spaces are incredibly rare. I'm always amazed at how the stone produces a kind of magic. The words we speak (whatever they are) take on a preciousness as the others all listen quietly. The words of others become tender and wise. The space between us fills up with empathy – we can really begin to understand what it's like for others in the circle to live their lives. (Often, this is much like it is for us to live our own lives. Sometimes, it is really not.)

I usually come away from these circles feeling warm and fuzzy. One night I can remember feeling resentful and tired afterwards. When I had my turn with the stone, I talked lightly about my week and what I was doing tomorrow.

What I should have said was: I really didn't want to come along to the listening circle tonight. I'm tired of people and their endless needs. I'm grumpy. I don't want to listen to anyone. Now leave me alone.

I don't know what would have happened next if I'd started with that. I might have felt more angry. I might have cried. I might have realised what the grumpiness was about. But I think it probably would have brought me closer to the people I was sitting with, rather than distancing me further.

Henri Nouwen, the Catholic priest, said: "Our society is so fragmented, our family lives so sundered by physical and emotional distance, our friendships so sporadic, our intimacies so 'in-between' things and often so utilitarian, that there are few places where we can feel truly safe."[11]

Safe spaces are scarce for most of us. Folks from oppressed groups can find it even more difficult to find a place where they can speak without fear of being judged, stereotyped or silenced. It's impossible for me to understand what it's like to be a person of colour in our racist world, or a trans person in our transphobic world. Spaces for, for example, women, people of colour or queer folk are crucial as we all continue to grapple with the parts of us that have been oppressed and the parts of us that (often unconsciously) collude with or actively take part in oppression. Even these extra-safe spaces are made up of human beings, and it's impossible to create an environment where we won't be occasionally offended, misunderstood, triggered or hurt.

Even when we find a safe-enough space, it's not easy to make use of them. It's not always appropriate to share what's in our heart – as a leader here at the temple, I sometimes need to be cautious about what I share so as not to dent the faith of other Sangha members. Often we are too afraid to show others what's really going on. I didn't share more honestly last night because I was scared – of being rejected, of hurting others. That's okay – that's how it is sometimes. Maybe I'll manage next time.

Our pockets of vulnerability can be deep, intense and fiercely protected. We need to go gently and be kind to ourselves. We can keep tiptoeing towards safe-enough spaces, and experimenting with sharing a little bit more of ourselves each time. When we do, we might just find the magic. As I write about it, I am getting a taste of it. The magic that arises in the circle is a warm and accepting tenderness. It is Amida's love.

Where are your safe spaces? How can you find more of them? How can you go gently and lean into them, just a tiny bit?

105

Grace

Satya

> I do not understand the mystery of grace – only that it meets us where we are and does not leave us where it found us. [12] ~ Anne Lamott

As I researched this chapter on grace, I got tangled up in theory. Who am I to say anything about grace? Is there even such a thing? How can I prove it or convince you? Does it always come through divine intervention? How does it all fit with the theology of Pure Land Buddhism? What would the scholars say?

I don't know what the scholars would say. All I can do is tell you how I use the concept of grace in my own life, and why it is as helpful to me as the knife that spreads jam on my toast.

Grace is the label I give to a phenomenon where something from outside of me gets inside me, often despite me, and which points me towards beauty, goodness and wisdom.

An example. Once when on retreat in France I was sitting in the shrine room during morning practice and feeling very alone. I asked for some sign from Amida that they were there – imagining that when they appeared they would fill me from my toes upwards with a warm cosy feeling. Nothing happened. Later, on a long walk in the burning midday sun across a flat landscape with no shady relief, just as I was running out of energy, a large tree came into view at the roadside. I stopped underneath it and lifted my face up to a cool breeze that seemed to come from nowhere. The coolness trickled over my face and body, bathing me in deliciousness. I didn't feel alone any more. I felt completely plugged into the divine. I laughed at myself for thinking I should be the one to decide when and how Amida would appear, and I felt a welling up of gratitude that so many good things were being offered to me all the time. The tears ran down my cheeks.

Grace isn't always a dramatic event. It may be spotting a tiny goldcrest with his streak-of-sunshine cap as we wander aimlessly in the garden, preoccupied by our small resentments. It may be that as we struggle with a particular relationship we hear a new author's name in several different places, and on buying their book discover exactly what we need to approach the relationship differently. It may be a strange feeling of security or shivers of joy that appear as we step into a cathedral.

Receiving grace leaves me lighter, less confused or hopeless and more full of faith. In my experience, having the word 'grace' in my vocabulary opens me up to more of these kinds of things happening again. It helps me to notice the things I'm not paying attention to, and to broaden the potential field from which grace may emerge.

Another quality of grace is that it reminds us of how much we receive and how little we have done to earn it. Every day most of us are provided with oxygen, a roof over our heads, food that has been grown and prepared by strangers, love from our friends and families. If we consider the transport we use to get to work – whether car, bus, bicycle or our own legs – we can list the knowledge and expertise necessary to build the vehicle, the raw materials given to us by the earth, the people who manufactured the pavements, the shop who sold our shoes, the people who paid for and built the roads, the traffic control systems, the emergency services when accidents happen... When we deeply reflect on what we receive and compare this to what we have offered in return, we realise that we would never be able to 'pay the world back' for what it has given us.

Fostering this kind of humility can be countercultural, but in my experience, feeling humble helps me to be open to receiving all the good stuff that life has to offer me. I'm not talking about the kind of humility that involves beating ourselves up or punishing ourselves. This self-punishment is just as much about ego as when we try to 'puff ourselves up' to feel better about ourselves. I'm talking more about a very realistic appraisal of our conditions and of our bombu nature, which leads to a natural sense of contrition. Contrition is one gate through which grace can enter.

So is grace some kind of divine intervention, something we receive from the buddhas? I don't know. What I do know is that the universe is vast and complex – beyond the limits of our imagination. If you laid the axons in your brain end to end they'd travel around the world four times. The sun is 15.6 million degrees Celsius at its core – a piece the size of a pinhead would give off enough heat to kill a person 160 kilometres away. If you put peanut butter under extreme high pressure, you can make diamonds from it. In my work as a psychotherapist, I never fail to be surprised and awed by the inner landscapes of my clients. In a world such as this, anything is possible.

Maybe grace is coincidence and wishful thinking, and maybe it is not. It doesn't matter. What matters is whether the concept of grace helps me to keep an open mind and heart, or not. It does. That is enough.

During my research I found a review of a book about grace by Anne Lamott. The reviewer said that Lamott's book was 'a field guide to looking for and recognising the gifts ... that are available to us, whatever our faith, when we open our hearts to that goodness of the universe which is currently beyond us.'[13] I love this description of the process of opening ourselves up to grace. It describes very well the leap of faith which is necessary to allow grace in. Can we remain soft and vulnerable, and let the buddhas help us?

I hope that you too might begin to find ways of opening your heart to the goodness of the universe which is currently beyond you. There's an infinite supply of it, just waiting to be invited inside.

Faith in faith

Kaspa

In his book Ocean, Kenneth Tanaka quotes Prof. Wilfred C. Smith's book Faith and Belief on the difference between these two ways of being:

"Faith is deeper, richer, more personal... It is an orientation of the personality, to oneself, to one's neighbour, to the universe; a total response. Belief, on the other hand, is the holding of certain ideas. Some might see it as the intellect's translation (even reduction?) of transcendence into ostensible terms."[14]

So belief is about ideas and ideals: the world was made like this, or like that; this is how to get to heaven; the spiritual world looks like this; so and so is true, other things are false.

A great deal of this kind of thinking appears to be about making people feel safe, rather than about genuine religious feeling. Human beings prefer certainties to uncertainties: if we know something, we can create a response to it that allows us to keep safe, either physically or psychologically.

It is much harder to keep steady, open hearted, and kind in the face of uncertainties, but this is what faith in faith asks us to do. It asks us to remain open and full of confidence in something we can't quite name, in the face of shifting circumstances and suffering.

In his book The Different Drum, M. Scott Peck talks about the four stages in a spiritual life. The first is chaotic, where people follow their whims and impulses and a certain selfish kind of freedom is the ideal. The second is institutional, where people have strong beliefs about right and wrong and the importance of following the rules. The third is sceptical, a movement into questioning beliefs and in which logic and the rational play an important role. Stage four is mystical, characterised by selflessness, and has its foundation in a genuine experience of something sacred that is not easily pinned down.

Belief is the domain of the institutional community, which offers certainty (and therefore safety) to those moving away from a chaotic life.

Faith is the domain of the mystic. It is an attitude or orientation which is more than a set of specific ideas. It is about entrustment to the benign presence of what we call Amida.

There may have been mystics in the Christian communities I grew up in, but it was belief that I was taught: follow the rules and all will be well. Mystics naturally tend to live good lives and keep the precepts, and so can appear similar in behaviour to those following the rules from a place of 'ought', but the spirit of their lives is different. Supported by their experience of being accepted just as they are, naturally they tend towards kindness.

In reality we are not simply at one stage or another, but rather some mix of all of them.

As a Christian child and then later as an atheist, surrounded by different kinds of belief, I judged myself and others. I repressed my queerness (for a long time). I repressed lots of other things too. Any thoughts or feelings that weren't acceptable were buried away. I became a well behaved child.

In communities of faith, and as my own faith deepened, I began to relax and feel more comfortable being myself.

Over time, it has become less clear exactly what I have faith in. In the chapter 'What is Amida?' I explore a few different explanations of what we are taking refuge in. I don't settle on a final answer.

This is faith in faith. Trusting an attitude of open heartedness. Trusting that there is something good I can take refuge in, whilst knowing I'll never completely describe what that is. It is not about arriving at an answer, or a place of certainty, but about a way of looking and a way of moving through the world.

Philip's story

Philip lives in Morecambe, joins us for practice on Zoom and regularly visits in person.

I had lived in Malvern and sometimes walked past the temple. Like a lot of people, I suspect, I had walked past and intended to go in but had never plucked up the courage to. Instead, I ended up living there a couple of years later for twelve months during a period of personal reflection and a feeling of something both human and spiritual missing in my life. I had dabbled in what might be described as spirituality, but confess I hadn't heard of Pure Land Buddhism.

Looking back now, I don't know if it was luck, some sort of divine intervention or fate as Pure Land Buddhism increasingly resonates with me at a deep level. Either way, I feel blessed. Being of a self-conscious and self-critical disposition, it has been a surprise to find opportunities such as chanting and prostrating with others have been particularly powerful for me.

Of course, things aren't always smooth. My (protective) 'parts' sometimes struggle to calmly and compassionately navigate the human interactions within a community of people. But that seems to be where a lot of the growth comes for me. I've often reflected with trusted others in the community about how special the opportunity to live and practice at Bright Earth is; somewhere safe enough to explore one's vulnerable human and neglected spiritual needs. I feel Pure Land Buddhism and Bright Earth are helping me know I am accepted 'just as I am'. And giving me an opportunity to take refuge, as well as cultivate deeper joy, humility and gratitude. Namo Amida Bu.

The Bodhisattva of Compassion

Satya

I talked about dukkha in a previous chapter. What else does Pure Land Buddhism have to say about suffering?

One of my favourite Buddhist stories features Quan Shi Yin (or Avalokiteshvara), the Bodhisattva of Compassion. Quan Yin means 'hearer of the cries of the world', and this bodhisattva vowed to work tirelessly to help all sentient beings until all of their suffering was extinguished. Of course, there is a lot of suffering. This legend says that Quan Yin became so overwhelmed by all this suffering that she shattered into a million pieces.

In the moment of shattering she cried out for help, and Amida Buddha came to her aid. He put her back together again and enabled her to continue helping. Quan Yin is often pictured with a little red Amida Buddha at her head, symbolising the fact that Amida is always there for her, and that she is never alone.

Although it's not possible for us to tune into all the suffering in the world at the same time, most of us can identify with Quan Yin's sense of being overwhelmed. Sometimes the suffering of others overwhelms us, no matter how hard we try to be patient or do the right thing. Just yesterday evening, not long after hearing about the death of a young activist I was very fond of, our evening meal didn't turn out as I had expected and hoped. My young parts zoned in on the meal as 'one more thing' they weren't in control of, and I was suddenly overwhelmed by grief for my friend, exacerbated by the wounding carried by my own young parts around not being able to control getting my needs met or being fed.

I take two things from the story of Quan Yin's shattering. The first is that we need to remember to ask for help. This begins with an admission that we can't do it on our own, and that even with an abundance of support we can't do it all. Even Quan Yin, the Bodhisattva of Compassion herself, found it too much to continue with her mission without the support of Amida. If Quan Yin needed help, then you can guarantee that this extremely limited human being does too!

The second is that when we know that we are held by a power greater than ourselves, we are able to find a new strength and it becomes possible to carry on. This strength or power isn't entirely ours – it belongs to Amida, and it comes through us. This could also be seen as faith – a knowing that we will be okay, and that we are being looked after, despite all the difficult things that happen to us and that happen in the world. When we have faith, we are more able to step out on a limb, and to experience the inevitable disappointments without losing heart.

Many of us, including me, don't find it easy to ask for help. In her book The Art of Asking, Amanda Palmer says:

"From what I've seen, it isn't so much the act of asking that paralyzes us – it's what lies beneath: the fear of being vulnerable, the fear of rejection, the fear of looking needy or weak. The fear of being seen as a burdensome member of the community instead of a productive one. It points, fundamentally, to our separation from one another."[15]

Maybe this is why Quan Yin put off asking for help until the moment of her shattering into a million pieces. I know from my own experience that it seems more possible to make myself ill or exhaust myself than it does to say to Kaspa, 'I'm overdoing it this week, can you help me with tomorrow's retreat?'

When we ask for help, we are letting go of the fantasy of an infinite source of self power. We are admitting how we are at the mercy of our fallible bodies, our frantic minds and the crashing waves of our emotions. We are acknowledging how dependent we are on a myriad of conditions beyond our control – our own histories, the people around us, the weather, the stock markets.... We are also, as Amanda Palmer says, opening ourselves up to rejection. It's much more comfortable for most of us to end up alone without having asked, rather than the awful rejection and loneliness of having asked and being told 'no'.

On the other hand, asking for help is the beginning of a spiritual life. It is the basis of the 12 step programmes, which emphasise the extreme difficulty of accepting the truth of the first step (admitting that we can't overcome our addictions on our own). It is also contained in the nembutsu – 'Namo' is our small self, calling out to the infinite power of Amida. Why would we need to say it if we were already the same as Amida? Why would we utter it in gratitude were it not to acknowledge our dependence on the buddhas and our happiness at being accepted and loved just as we are?

Practising Buddhism doesn't result in a complete eradication of suffering in our lives or in the lives of others. It is pretty upfront in saying, whatever you do, you will continue to experience discomfort and pain. What it does give us is a broader context in which to contain this suffering. It encourages us to lean on the Buddha, Dharma and Sangha in order to receive comfort, courage and blessings. It inspires us to continue living our lives as nobly as we can. Maybe there is some ultimate point to all this suffering – maybe there isn't. There is a lot that we don't know. But in the meantime we can remember that Amida is holding us and, if necessary, will put us back together again if we just call out and ask.

The Buddha of measurelessness

Kaspa

In the Larger Pure Land Sutra, the text which describes Amida creating his Pure Land of Love and Bliss, there is a section which describes the various names of Amida. It says that:

Amitayus is, therefore, called
the Buddha of Measureless Light – Amitabha;
the Buddha of Boundless Light;
the Buddha of Unimpeded Light;
the Buddha of Incomparable Light;
the Buddha of the Light of the Monarch of Fires;
the Buddha of Pure Light;
the Buddha of the Light of Joy;
the Buddha of the Light of Wisdom;
the Buddha of Continuous Light;
the Buddha of Inconceivable Light;
the Buddha of Ineffable Light; and
the Buddha of Light Outshining the Sun and the Moon.

This list gives us some sense of what it is that we are taking refuge in when we take refuge in Amida. Throughout the sutra, light is used as a metaphor for both love and wisdom. We sometimes still use it that way in English – someone who is in love is 'all lit up', for example, and a new or expectant mother is 'glowing'. Enlightenment – in the non-Buddhist sense – means to become wise. We have lightbulb moments. The twelve kinds of light in this list give us some idea of the qualities of wise-love that Amida has for us.

The Buddha's love is measureless. It does not measure: we are loved whatever we do and whoever we are. The ideal parent has this kind of deep love for their child. It is unbreakable, regardless of what the child does – the child is not measured by the parent. As well as not measuring, the love of the Buddha is so vast that it cannot be measured.

The Buddha's love is boundless and unimpeded. It does not stop at the edge of the Pure Land but goes on and on. We draw lines around our conditional human love. We love our family, but exclude others. Or we love our country, but not other countries. The light of the Buddha is not like this; there is nothing you can put between yourself and the Buddha that will stop the Buddha loving you (although we do sometimes refuse to acknowledge the light, when it does reach us).

The Buddha's love is incomparable. It does not love some beings more and others less, and the light itself is beyond comparison. The love of the Buddha is far above and beyond other loves. When we love another person there are all sorts of conditions attached, some conscious, some unconscious. I'll love you as long as you keep loving me, or I'll love you if you agree this is the kind of person I am, or as long as you don't misbehave, or any number of other things. A good relationship moves in the direction of unconditional love, but never gets there. In human love we find people whose conditional love is a good fit for our own. The love of the Buddha asks nothing of us.

The Buddha's love is like the monarch of fires. If one great fire is the source of all fire in the world, the flame from which all candles are lit, then we can think of all love as reflections of the Buddha's love. We are able to love to the extent that we have felt the Buddha's love (although we may call this love by many different names). The love we feel and encounter in this world is like moonlight, shining clear and bright, but always a reflection of a much greater light.

The love of the Buddha is pure. Our own love has met disappointment, and so is held back or contaminated by fear, or guilt, or anger. The Buddha's love is not affected by disappointment; it keeps on loving, clean and pure, like a spring that never runs dry.

The Buddha's love is joyful and wise. This describes the kind of love the Buddha has for us. It celebrates our successes and it celebrates us just being who we are – the Buddha's love is always pleased to see us. The Buddha is wise; they can see the whole of who we really are, even when we cannot. Buddhism is a path of transformation and the Buddha knows what is best for us, and longs for it, but loves us wherever we are on or off that path.

The Buddha's love is continuous. It does not stop, whatever we do.

Despite all of the words I have used to describe it, the Buddha's love is inconceivable and ineffable. We make it smaller in order to talk about it. We make it smaller in order to feel it. It is deeper and more vast than the most powerful spiritual experiences suggest.

The light of the Buddha outshines the sun and the moon. These were the brightest lights at the time the sutra was composed, and perhaps we can imagine stronger lights now, brighter stars. The Buddha's light outshines these too. And even if we can imagine brighter stars, we cannot even look directly at our own sun without being blinded.

This is what we are taking refuge in when we take refuge in Amida. There is no space between us and Amida. We talk about calling out to the Buddha, but they are always right here.

Maria's story

Maria is a project management professional in a construction consultancy, in the energy & utilities sector. She is an amateur harpist and is training to become a Buddhist minister at Bright Earth.

On my first-ever visit to Malvern in between the lockdowns (my husband Steve and I lived in Birmingham at the time) I noticed there was a lovely Buddhist temple on Worcester Road. Unfortunately we couldn't visit the temple itself due to the Covid restrictions. However I was already contemplating moving to Malvern, and realising there was a Buddhist temple here sped up that decision for me! We moved to Malvern in early July 2021 and visited the temple on an open day about a month later. Steve and I were both overwhelmed by the warm welcome and also appreciated the "down-to-Earth" style at Bright Earth (fits the name!) that was easy to connect to and empathise with, no matter your background and relationship with Buddhism. My personal relationship with Pure Land Buddhism and Bright Earth has been growing and deepening ever since and I am delighted to have met a whole new family of the lovely people in the Sangha.

When I first visited the temple, I didn't even consider myself strictly speaking "Buddhist", more like "empathising" or "interested". I've been practising meditation on my own for a long time and I read a few books on the Dharma. However, coming to the practice at Bright Earth and having my own practice, learning more about the Pure Land tradition in the book groups and experiencing the warmth and support of the Sangha during the difficult times convinced me that this was the right path for me. I've realised that the change that I went through is open to anyone and it would be a great blessing to share the path with others and support them. I am now part of the Living the Dharma programme and among the first cohort of Bright Earth minister trainees!

My own practice is very simple and has to work around my busy schedule – however even a very short practice can make a huge change. I practice gassho – the tradition I started with particular emphasis on getting less frustrated at work and more accepting of the people I might find hard to deal with. I also practice nembutsu and meditation, especially now that I've set up a lovely little "dahlia shrine" in my garden which is a joy to be in! I use a bespoke "music mala" with my harp practice – one made by the lovely Kusuma who also makes malas for the temple. I was also introduced to Internal Family Systems (IFS) through the temple book groups – an approach I've used fairly regularly since to tackle deep psychological questions, including the anxiety around separation from my family due to the ongoing war in Ukraine.

I find the practice has been gradually helping me to be more accepting and patient with myself and the people around me; both Steve and I have also been gradually making changes to our lifestyles to make sure our ways are more sustainable and environmentally friendly.

I feel blessed that Bright Earth is part of my life now and I am very grateful to Satya, Kaspa and the other Bright Earth ministers, as well as the Sangha, for making this possible.

Other power

Satya

I like to think that I have at least some control over most aspects of my life. I work hard so I will earn enough money or get praise, I eat healthily so I won't get ill, and I behave in particular ways around my friends and family so they'll like me, see me in a particular way, and do what I want them to do...

Alas, sometimes I receive criticism, not praise, however hard I work. Sometimes I get ill, despite how much I exercise and how healthily I eat. And the people I love (and those I don't love) have a very annoying habit of not doing the things I'd prefer them to do.

Co-dependents Anonymous (CoDA) is a 12 step programme for people who have codependent parts – parts that try to make things safe by trying to control or please others. This group has a lot to offer when it comes to helping us acknowledge the extent of our powerlessness over people, places and things. The first of the 12 steps of CoDA is: 'Admitted we were powerless over others, and that our lives had become unmanageable.'

Most of us are at least a teensy bit codependent. Codependency is what happens when we make ourselves into a Higher Power, deciding that it's our job to direct or manipulate others for their own good (that is, for our own good). It is also what happens when we make other people into our Higher Power, relying so completely on their acceptance or approval of us that we'll do whatever it takes to get it. These behaviours are totally understandable. When they are extreme, they can also result in problems or total havoc as we try harder and harder to influence others in various ways.

One example from my own life is how I feel around people who are in chaos. Part of the legacy of having lived with an alcoholic for many years is that I can feel unsafe around people who are in denial or acting in chaotic ways. When I encounter people in chaos I do all kinds of things to try and get them to pay attention to their chaos and to start healing it or sorting it out. I might suggest that they seek therapy or encourage them to go to a 12 step programme. I might point out to them how their actions are affecting others. On the surface it might look like these things are for their benefit, but when I make these suggestions more than once and keep making them, my other motivation becomes clearer. I actually want these people to go into therapy for my own benefit, so that they can sort out their chaos and I can feel safer around them. It's not just about what's best for them.

Most of our behaviour towards others will contain a mix of both self-protective (codependent) and selfless motivations. Codependent behaviour happens because, usually for some historical reason, there is something that we are afraid of. We may not have any awareness of this fear at all, but it still drives us to behave in ways that aren't in our best interests or in the best interests of others. Examples are people who stay in unsatisfactory relationships because they are afraid of being alone, people who bully others because they are afraid of being vulnerable or 'less than' others, or people who are demanding because they are afraid of being rejected.

As with all compulsive behaviour we often start in denial about the true impact of our codependency on ourselves and others. This is partly because letting go of the denial would also mean letting go of the control (which of course we never actually have to begin with!). To get to the first step, admitting that we are powerless over others, we usually have to bash up against the consequences of our behaviour repeatedly until it gets painful enough to admit that something isn't working.

Some people reach the first step after the break-up of a string of romantic relationships, some after intractable issues with friends, and some after realising that they are putting up with things that they shouldn't be putting up with in relationships. Reaching the first step is often a mixture of anguish, as we face the chaos we've created in our lives for many years and begin to take responsibility for it, and a release, as we let go of some of the denial that takes such a lot of energy to maintain. It can be a relief to see the naked truth of our situation.

In a similar way, Pure Land Buddhism reminds us that we don't have as much control over the world as we would like to believe. We are all bombu – foolish beings of wayward passion – and we are blown like long grass in the wind by these often-hidden passions. Our passions (greed, hate and delusion, and the fear behind these impulses) drive us to act in self-protective ways, which ultimately cause us trouble.

Pure Land Buddhism suggests that often these passions are just too big for us – it is impossible for us to control them. We might try to curb our greed from a position of self power, by limiting how many glasses of wine we drink or by trying hard not to lose our temper at people, and we can keep some of our passions under control for some of the time, but sooner or later we encounter the depth of our various compulsions and limitations and we realise how fruitless it is to believe that we can perfect ourselves if only we try hard enough.

We not only have limited control over our own behaviour and the behaviour of others, but also over material objects, money, the weather, our physical surroundings, and of course how and when we're going to die. This is what the Buddha realised when he experienced the Four Sights – we're not in control of how quickly we age or when we get sick either.

In my experience, when I acknowledge the reality of my situation – impermanence and my limited nature – it offers me an opportunity to surrender to the other power of Amida Buddha. I see myself as I am, a vulnerable and fallible being, and I turn to the infinite love and wisdom of something bigger. This 'something bigger' exists, in my experience, both outside of me and inside me. I surrender every time I say the nembutsu: Namo, little me, calling out to Amida Buddha for courage and for consolation.

Acknowledging our dependence and our frailty is not always comfortable for us Westerners. Other power approaches are not popular.

They strip us of our comfortable illusions of self-control, and they ask us to hand ourselves over to something we might not even believe in or understand. Why should I trust this 'Higher Power' more than I trust myself? This reluctance is often compounded by our disappointing or downright damaging experiences of religion, and our past experience of being let down by other people. We learn that being self-sufficient is the safest way to be. We also use the 'firefighter' parts of us like alcoholic parts, disordered eating parts or workaholic parts to avoid our vulnerabilities. Our self-protective defences do a great job for us, and they are understandably reluctant to relax or stand down.

There are different ways of softening or breaking through this self-protection. One way is more painful – known as the 'rock bottom' of recovery when the addict, after years of pain and chaos, finally admits that they are not in control of their life and calls out for help. We might also be lucky enough to have our defences more gently worn away by compassion – by the healing power of nature or animals, or by the loyal care of friends or family. However it happens, we become clear: this way isn't working, and we need help. We are ready to try something different.

Putting ourselves into the care of a Higher Power – Amida Buddha, or however you conceptualise something that is bigger than you and knows better than you – is how we take refuge. We no longer rely on ourselves to know all the answers or to know best, including knowing what is best for ourselves. We open our eyes and ears to the wisdom that the Universe might be offering us. We hand problems over when they are too big or confusing for us, and we wait patiently to be shown a different solution. We develop our relationship with our Higher Power by listening (spending time in quiet meditation or chanting) and speaking to them (making offerings, expressing gratitude or asking for help). We begin to feel that we are not alone.

In my experience, once I had released myself (or had been released) from the tyranny of thinking-I-could-control-everything, the relief was huge. Of course, our self-protection will always be there. We need self-protection! I often catch myself trying to manipulate the outcome of a situation, or getting compulsive around the internet. I am a work in progress. I admit my powerlessness every time I say Namo Amida Bu.

The good news is that whenever we catch sight of our self-protective ego, we have an opportunity. These moments are gates which allow grace through. Amida will find a way to gently work on us, despite our self-protection's best attempts to thwart them. We just say Namo Amida Bu, and the Buddha takes care of the rest.

Kusumavarsa's story

Kusumavarsa is Buddhist minister and unpaid Carer, and a mala maker.

I first found Buddhism (or maybe it found me) while at Art college in 1989. One dusty old book that I don't think had been loaned in years. I took it out for a week and promptly returned it having not understood a word of it. For the next 15 years I skirted around Buddhism, taking Yoga classes, learning meditation, and practising Reiki.

In 2004 when I took a job as a Complementary Therapy Coordinator at a hospice, the same questions came up time and time again: "What do you believe in?" "What becomes of us when we die?" Patients who came to see me for therapy were afraid and looking for answers.

I read an introductory book on Buddhism and the pieces of the puzzle started to fit together. The four noble truths and the eight fold path felt like the remedy for the self driven world I was living in. Out of a desire to help others cope with the suffering life brought them I began studying Buddhist Psychology.

In June 2010 I was immersed in Buddhist Psychology alongside training to be a chaplain with the Amida Order. Little did I know that everything I theorised and practised would become such a lifeline for myself when my twins were born 13 weeks early. I went through a traumatic labour and both children have lifelong disabilities.

That lesson in impermanence has never left me, and having disabled children teaches you how to be present with each day and all the ups and downs that it might bring. From the moment they were born I was thrust into a world of unpaid care. It's a very silent, invisible world. Having the nembutsu to anchor me, and Amida to lean into brings a feeling of unconditional love for which I feel immense gratitude.

At the age of 50 I was diagnosed with ADHD and Autism; finally an answer to my lifelong quirkiness! This news has also brought a new dimension to my practice as a Buddhist. Meditation and nembutsu are great at helping to increase dopamine levels, something that is lacking in those of us with ADHD. So there I was for years giving myself self care without even knowing it.

I carry Amida with me daily, as it is after all a heart's practice. Who doesn't want to live gently with a kind heart? I practice nembutsu while mala making: I practice nembutsu while weeding my garden with its view of the Malvern Hills. This is the way of the Pure Land Buddhist, nembutsu helps to cultivate a love that with time slowly drips into everything you do.

Compassion for you, compassion for all living beings. Just as you are.

Spiritual training

Kaspa

When I first moved into The Buddhist House I was classified as a trainee. There were certain formal things I had to learn before becoming ordained – how to perform certain ceremonies and so on – but being a trainee is also about learning, or taking on board, a certain kind of spirit.

In the community a spiritual trainee also learnt very practical things: how to cater for large groups of people, how to take care of a property and a garden. Trainees were taken to the edge of their comfort zone for the powerful learning that can happen there.

The spirit of that training was something about faith, something about open handedness, and something about a willingness to do what's best for the community, rather than just for oneself.

We could also talk about spiritual training as bodhisattva training; it is learning how to love more deeply, and to create the conditions in which others can love more deeply.

When we frame it in this way we can see that a mixture of practical and emotional learning will be part of the process. Love needs to manifest in practical ways in the world, and some of the ways in which we are called to serve love will naturally take us to the edge of our comfort zones, which can bring up all sorts of fears and defences.

Learning how to relate to the emotions that appear in this space is an important part of spiritual or bodhisattva training.

You don't need to be on the road to ordination to be a spiritual trainee. Buddhism, including Pure Land Buddhism, holds that spiritual training is a good thing for everyone to do. Or perhaps we could say that it is inevitable – once we have taken refuge in the Buddha, spiritual training will happen naturally.

As we feel loved and held by the Buddha and the Sangha, some of our defences drop away and our loving heart will want to express itself. We'll take some loving action which will be more or less successful, and our training begins. At some point our compassionate action will fail – either we'll be unskilful, or we'll simply meet a practical limit. If we can remember refuge in this moment we can experience being held by the Buddha in the midst of the difficulty, and then naturally we'll want to go back into the world and be compassionate again.

One of the first times I was asked to be in charge of catering for a large group at The Buddhist House, I had a moment of being overwhelmed. I was struggling to imagine how I could produce food for all of these people that were coming. All sorts of defences and thought processes were being triggered. What if no-one liked what I made? (Or what if just one person didn't like it?) What if I spent too much money? I was exposing myself to being judged and this felt like an extremely dangerous place to be. If anything went wrong it had the potential to trigger a shame spiral. Ironically, fear of that spiral and the worries it created caused their own problems.

I was frozen and I couldn't imagine taking the first step. I couldn't even imagine what the first step should be.

I knocked on the door of my then teacher's office. I could see that he was deep in the midst of work, but he called me in anyway. I nervously laid out my practical problems. I didn't speak of the fear of being judged: after all what if I was judged for having those fears? He just listened and nodded.

I was expecting some practical advice, either some guidance around the cooking, or an approach to take, or even to be sent to someone else who could help.

Instead he said, 'Okay.' He was smiling warmly.

I got the message. This was my problem to solve. I didn't like that message so much at the time. What I saw later was that simple, 'okay', was an act of faith.

It was an act of faith in my ability to solve this problem myself, and more importantly an act of faith in something greater: that even if the food didn't appear when it should have done, or wasn't up to scratch, or I blew the budget for the whole week on take-away food, this wouldn't be the whole story.

Any failure would be held by the Buddha. I could then look at what had happened from a position of feeling loved rather than judged, and learn something not only about catering, but about failure and the human condition too. Or perhaps I could even take the next step and go beyond adequacy and inadequacy to simply dwelling in reality.

The catering went well, no one starved and most people enjoyed the food. Although I'm not sure how they felt about the cauliflower and almond soup that ended up tasting like liquid marzipan.

John Daido Loori said that the teacher's job is to pull the rug from under the spiritual trainee, and then to encourage them and help them to get back up again.[16]

I'm not sure we need to worry too much about pulling the rug from underneath our trainees or from under each other – life does that often enough anyway. What is important is to keep trusting in the presence of Amida, regardless of what else is happening, and to trust that there is a place beyond success and failure. A place where we are accepted just as we are.

A Buddhist approach to self-care

Satya

Did the Buddha want us to look after ourselves? There is a particular ideal in Western Buddhism around denying our own needs and limitations, either in the service of others or as a 'spiritual quest'. In the past this narrative unhelpfully hooked into my own personal psychology, which holds that I should always attend to others before I attend to myself. A few years ago I began to question this approach, which comes from my dysfunction rather than from a place of spacious compassion, which produces mixed results for those I am 'helping', and which often leads me to burn-out. Instead I began to look for support for the idea of self-care in the Buddhist texts.

It was important for me to find a story in the Samyutta Nikaya called the Sedaka Sutta, or the Bamboo Acrobat[17]. In the story, our bamboo acrobat climbs onto his bamboo pole and asks his assistant Medakathalika to come and stand on his shoulders. She does so (I can imagine them precariously balancing) and then he says to her, 'You look after me, dear Medakathalika, and I will look after you – thus with us looking after each other, guarding one another, we'll show off our craft, receive some payment, and safely climb down the bamboo pole.' At this Medakathalika says, 'That will not do at all, Master! You look after yourself, master, and I will look after myself. Thus with each of us looking after ourselves, guarding ourselves, we'll show off our craft, receive some payment, and safely climb down from the bamboo pole. That's the right way to do it!'

If the bamboo acrobat had indeed focussed too much on Medakathalika, he would have neglected to attend to his own balance and, in falling off the tall pole, would endanger her life. The Buddha is showing us that we have a responsibility to tend to our own balance – whether this be physical, psychological or spiritual – in order to keep ourselves steady. If we are steady, we will be able to support others. This story is the Buddha's version of the instructions you will find on the oxygen masks in aeroplanes – in case of emergency, put on your own mask before you put on your children's.

Of course, sometimes we are required to put our own needs aside and tend to someone else's before our own. If our child is sick and needs to go to the hospital, it doesn't matter if we are hungry or exhausted – we do what needs to be done. There are no hard and fast rules in life. Sometimes we need a teaching that helps us to tend more carefully to our own bodies or well-being, and sometimes we need a teaching that encourages us to look beyond our ego in order to let something from outside penetrate our tangles of self-protection.

In the story of the Bamboo Acrobat, the Buddha seems to be encouraging us to become mindful of our own balance using a self power approach. We notice whether we are off-balance and we then take the appropriate action to put ourselves back in balance.

We can also access compassion through other power, by reciting the nembutsu. In every recitation we are acknowledging our limited selves, calling out (Namo) and hearing the response of Amida (Amida Bu) which is to love and accept us, and others, just as we are. Whether we see Amida as some higher part of ourselves, like buddha nature, or as completely outside of ourselves, or as a mixture of both, the nembutsu can give us access to a source of compassion that we wouldn't usually have access to.

Sometimes we undervalue ourselves as a part of our habitual patterns of behaviour. One of my patterns is to refuse help from others. This is related to taking care of the other person before I take care of myself. Part of me believes that I can't trust others to look after themselves, and so if I don't look after them, they may neglect themselves to the extent that they are then unable to look after me. In this way, attending to them first is (in part) a convoluted way of getting my own needs met. Recently one of our templemates offered to take some mugs into the kitchen and wash them up. I found myself saying 'no thanks, I'll do them', as I subconsciously attempted to protect him from over-offering and becoming resentful, or burning himself out, or who knows what. I managed to catch myself and I took it back, telling him that actually I would very much like him to wash up the mugs.

Using Internal Family Systems and working with these parts of me has been hugely helpful in terms of helping these parts of me to relax and trust that they don't need to keep such a close eye on other people. Also, the behaviour of these parts of me are very deeply ingrained – there may be a limit to how much change is possible. This is where other power comes in. When we bash up against our limits, whether this is a simple acknowledgement of our current levels of self-protection, or being realistic about the limits of future change, we can feel loved by Amida just the same. This love soaks into us and reaches parts of us that we would never be able to reach through our willed efforts. We are putting ourselves into relationship with the Infinite. When I sit in the shrine room and make an offering of my disturbed thoughts or my disappointment in myself to the Buddha, I am giving these thoughts and feelings away. In return I receive a sense of peace and settled faith – it soaks into me as fine rain gradually soaks the dry earth.

As well as putting others before myself, I also find it difficult to acknowledge my limits (until I bash up against them with some force). This is another way of keeping myself safe – if I have a limitless capacity to contain others and keep going, then I never need to fear that I will be dependent on (unreliable) others. I also never need fear that I will fail to meet the needs of others, which would lead to them falling into chaos and threatening my own safety.

Shantideva has some useful advice for me (and maybe you) in this regard, in the following verses from Shantideva's Way of the Bodhisattva:

47

First of all I should examine well what is to be done
To see whether I can pursue it or cannot undertake it.
(If I am unable) it is best to leave it,
But once I have started I must not withdraw.

67

When my strength declines, I should leave whatever I am doing
In order to be able to continue with it later.
Having done something well, I should put it aside
With the wish (to accomplish) what will follow.[18]

So – decide whether or not we have the energy to do something
before we begin, and if we can't continue, put it aside and finish it later.
Great practical advice from the 8th century!

Another thing that helps me to give myself permission to look
after myself is remembering that even the Buddha rested when he was
feeling ill or tired. Sometimes his attendant Ananda would turn visitors
away in order to preserve the Buddha's energy. It is permissible to rest
when we need to rest – not just permissible, but advisable. This is a
simple lesson that I need to relearn over and over, as I catch myself
pushing myself beyond my capacity or feeling terrible about myself when
I am no longer able to contain the emotion of another. As I said earlier I
also find Jesus' words a helpful reminder – 'For my yoke is easy and my
burden is light.'[19] If I listen out for Amida's wishes for me, I won't be
asked to do everything for everyone else all the time. I can listen to my
limits and care for this body and mind of mine – just as I care for the
minds and bodies of other beings.

Amida, help me to find the middle way, as Shakyamuni Buddha
found after he was saved from self-starvation by Sujata the milkmaid.
Help me to care for others and to care for myself with the exact same
loving tenderness. Help me to forgive others, and to forgive myself.

Trusting

Kaspa

When we take refuge we put our trust in the Buddha, Dharma, and Sangha. Earlier I talked about living a faith-filled life. Putting our trust in these three things is the same thing: a faith-filled life is a life in which we trust that following the Dharma will lead to the best outcomes, or trusting that the Buddha has our best interests at heart without knowing exactly what those best interests are.

We can trust the Buddha and the Dharma completely, but how much can we trust human beings? Regardless of where we are in our spiritual journey there are times when we all act from greed, hate and delusion.

A few years ago some friends of the Sangha came to visit the temple. It was their first visit. A few of us were in the garden working. It was a beautiful sunny afternoon. These friends came down into the garden to spend some time with us. We had cups of tea and cake, and we talked about all sorts of things. On their way out they went through the temple and collected their bags which they'd left in the hallway. A purse had gone missing from one of the bags.

They retraced their steps through the town, calling in at the shops they had stopped in, despite being sure that their purse was in the bag when they arrived at the temple.

The temple front door had been on the latch all afternoon. There had been a group using the shrine room, and the shrine room door had been propped open in the afternoon. The shrine room is next to the front door and for a while we tried to tell ourselves that no one could have come into the temple through the front door without the people in the shrine room noticing. When the purse didn't turn up anywhere else it began to look likely that it had been taken from the bag when it was in our hallway. Of course someone could have opened the door quietly and slipped in without anyone noticing – the group in the shrine room were concentrating on their own activities, not who was coming and going through the rest of the building.

I was shaken at the idea of someone coming into the temple and helping themselves to something that wasn't theirs. This is my home as well as a Buddhist temple. I have always wanted to model trusting people here, from giving people responsibility for different jobs to having a donation bowl that's open rather than a slot into a secure box.

A few years ago something like this might have led me to trust people less, but trusting people has become important to me.

A few days before the theft I'd been reading Amanda Palmer's The Art of Asking[20] and she relates a similar story. After years of trusting fans and having that trust rewarded, someone took advantage of that trust in a way that was much more violent and invasive than having a purse taken. She went through a process of questioning how much she should trust people again and then realised that all acts of entrusting (entrusting in samsara, anyway) entail risk. If it's a sure thing we don't really need to trust at all, not in the same way as when we take a chance on someone or something less known.

If we trust ordinary people, sometimes we will be disappointed, and sometimes we will be rewarded. In my experience the more we trust, the more that trust is rewarded. If we go into the world believing that people are generally full of goodwill, we will see and receive much more goodwill than if we enter the world with a suspicious attitude. I don't think that's just confirmation bias – I think people are much more likely to be warm and friendly and willing to help if you are open hearted and think well of them. If you approach someone already believing they are going to rip you off, or let you down somehow, what do you think will happen?

Amanda Palmer decided to keep on trusting people, and so did I.

I want to encourage goodwill and open heartedness in the people around me, and if I approach them with suspicion and end up inspiring small mindedness and meanness it doesn't really feel like I'm doing my job properly.

As a Buddhist priest and spiritual teacher, I want the people around me to be the best and most loving they can be, and that means creating the conditions in which that is more likely to happen, not less likely.

Having said that, I make sure that there's never more cash than I'm willing to lose in the open donation bowl, and we do keep it inside the temple and not out on the street. Along with being trusted, there's something else which inspires people to be trustworthy: having a relationship with the person doing the trusting.

I'd be surprised if it was someone from the temple community who took the purse. We're much less likely to rip someone off if we have a personal connection with them, if we know who they are, and if we like them. It's not a cast iron guarantee of course, but if we cultivate good relationships, and trust the people we are relating to, we're much more likely to have that trust rewarded than if we just leave our purse on a train in the middle of a busy city where we don't know anyone.

Although of course, as Satya will tell you, given her experience of losing her purse on the London underground and getting it back on the same day, there are plenty of strangers who are trustworthy too.

Some people need to learn to trust others more, and some need to learn to trust others less. Trust should be coupled with discernment and an awareness of potential risks.

If your early experience of people was that they fulfilled all of your needs and were completely reliable, it can come as a shock to encounter greed, hate and delusion, and the limitations of ordinary human beings. If we trust people more than they are trustworthy, we can end up supporting their patterns of dysfunction as they take advantage of us. We can end up getting hurt.

We can't control whether our trust will be rewarded or not. Sometimes we do nothing and people are kind to us, sometimes we pour all of our energy into a relationship and we get burned. All the same I'm going to keep trusting the people in my community, and looking for the goodwill in strangers.

Our biggest addiction

Satya

One way of talking about Buddhist philosophy is as a theory of addiction. We all develop addictions as attempts at avoiding the realities of impermanence, pain and loss. We want to hang onto the good stuff, push the bad stuff away and remain ignorant of the stuff that confuses us. As a child we might steal a chocolate biscuit after being told off and as we eat it, we notice that the knot in our stomach feels better. When we feel the knot again, we seek out biscuits. All kinds of compulsive behaviours develop in this way – from the relatively benign (watching television, keeping too busy) to the potentially fatal (drug addiction, eating disorders).

We all have our pet addictions, but what is our favourite? When I was ordained as a Buddhist priest in 2011 my first name changed from Fiona to Satyavani – Satya for short. For the first few months, when people said my new name it was invisible to me. They had to repeat it several times, getting steadily louder, in order to get my attention. Now when someone says 'Satya' I hear it immediately – even if the word is nestled in a hubbub of noise. It's like your dog hearing the word 'walkies'!

I notice the same effect when I look at photos of a friend's wedding and find a photo with me in it. Sometimes we may be drawn towards looking at ourselves and admiring ourselves, and at other times we may feel dismayed, thinking that we look too big or unattractive. Sometimes we just want to check what our dress or our faces look like! Either way, our selves draw our attention very powerfully.

This attraction to (or avoidance of) anything related to ourselves goes deep and it makes up the bulk of many of our preoccupations. When we are listening to others we might relate what they're saying to our own lives, and plan what we want to say as soon as they stop talking. We surround ourselves with people, objects and activities that support our identity – wearing clothes that signify 'who we are' to the world and joining various gangs (football team supporters, Buddhist Sanghas...) We love our mobile phones and social media because they often point back towards me, me, me.

Why are we so preoccupied with our selves? Why do we invest so much time and energy in building ourselves up? Before I explore this I want to pose another question.

Is there such a thing as a permanent self to 'build up' anyway? This is where Buddhism messes with our heads! There are various meditations in the Buddhist canon which invite us to have an experience of the insubstantial and ever-changing nature of our selves. One meditation asks us to focus our attention in turn on the gases, liquids and solids entering and leaving our bodies. After years or even months, how much remains of us that was the same substance as it was before? Another meditation instructs us to imagine our bodies after we have died, and to see clearly that we will dissolve back into the earth and disappear completely.

We might think that our personalities are here to stay, but if we look more closely we find that although we have habit patterns that are deeply ingrained, they are also all subject to change. We all know people who have completely turned their lives around, and dropped all kinds of destructive behaviours that had seemed to be an integral part of them. This happens in reverse too, when people have mental crises or fall into serious addiction. Some of us know what it feels like to fall in love or have a baby or to be given a serious medical diagnosis – the things that were previously important can change overnight. Many of us explore familiar themes for long periods of our lives – being retriggered to remember the abandonment we experienced as a small child, experiencing repeated disappointment in our career, or trying to find a way of overcoming specific issues in our marriage or friendships, but even these 'groundhog day' experiences change very slightly every time we encounter them.

If there is no such thing as a permanent self and our 'self' is the vehicle we find ourselves travelling in, it's no wonder that we invest a considerable amount of energy into patching up the holes and making it as 'solid' as we can. We often use our stories about ourselves as our armour – maybe we buy into the illusion that we are self-sufficient and in control of everything that happens to us, or maybe we feel completely helpless and so refuse to take any action at all. We take refuge in our physical bodies and our personalities as if they will always be there.

Another common characteristic of us human beings is that we don't deal very well with the unknown. It's usually more comfortable for us to jump to conclusions about what is happening rather than live with extended periods of uncertainty. We like to have some certainty about 'who we are' – for example, I am someone who can't draw, and I am a cat person. When I'm presented with evidence that counters these theories, for example I am asked to do a sketch and it turns out okay, or I bond with a friend's dog, I ignore this evidence as it doesn't fit neatly with the identity I have chosen for myself, or which I've grown into by default.

This mechanism works well in that it keeps us from feeling confused about who we are, and it gives us a measure of security. The downside is that it takes a lot of energy to keep repressing all the experiences which are counter to our personalities as we think we know them, and we also miss out on a big portion of life-as-it-actually-is, because there is no space for it in our conception of ourselves. As an example, in the years since the first edition of this book, I discovered that I am actually a dog person. Our two little dogs are at the centre of my life, and I can't imagine a future without a doggie companion. If I'd clung onto my 'cat person' identity I would have missed out on so much.

The Dharma, the teachings of Buddhism, helps us to loosen our addiction to the illusion of a permanent self. If we can begin to loosen this addiction, we will not only free up the energy we've been using to keep the truth at bay, but we'll also have access to more truth about ourselves and about the world. As the psychotherapist Carl Rogers said,

'The facts are always friendly, every bit of evidence one can acquire, in any area, leads one that much closer to what is true.'[21] It is better for us to know that we are sometimes good at drawing, as it opens us up to a creative hobby that we never thought would be possible. It's also better for us to know that when we hold space for other people it takes energy from us, as we can then be realistic about how much space we can offer, book in rest time after big events, and be curious about why we are like this and what parts of us might appreciate some loving attention.

Sitting with the truth of our impermanent selves can be uncomfortable. We have to develop a capacity for 'negative capability', that useful phrase first used by the poet Keats which describes '...when a man is capable of being in uncertainties, Mysteries, doubts, without any irritable reaching after fact & reason...'[22] How do we get better at negative capability? By taking refuge in something that is more permanent than our selves – by taking refuge in the three jewels of Buddha, Dharma and Sangha.

Taking refuge allows us to feel that we are held, regardless of who we are or of what might happen. As our faith grows, our capacity for negative capability will increase. We will gradually get to know those parts of ourselves which have been hiding in the shadows, and we will become more intimate with the world too. Dharma is the truth of things-as-they-are. We are fallible beings and our bodies and our personalities are ever-changing. This doesn't mean that we can't enjoy being in our bodies right now, as they hold us upright and allow us to see the beautiful world. It doesn't mean we can't enjoy our quirks and preferences, without taking ourselves too seriously. Here we are. Let's make the most of it.

Alison's story

Alison lives in the Bright Earth temple – she is making a new start in her life, and her life is full of new beginnings.

I first visited Bright Earth temple about six years ago, on a visit to Malvern to see a friend. I loved the warm feeling in the temple and the hills and finding myself walking in the hills I had a strong feeling that I had come home. It was a strange thing, as I'd spent two decades overseas before reluctantly relocating to England. I visited a number of times and experienced the same feeling each time. After the very long Covid lockdown I visited again and found it very difficult to get away, missing my train! I returned to London and restarted the nembutsu, this time very devotedly, and kept the practice going. There was talk of me moving into the temple but I couldn't see a way. One day I had a huge heart opening experience and knew that I was to move to the temple and Malvern and shortly after, the opportunity came as I was forced to suddenly relocate. Although a bit sudden, everything just fell into place. It has been by no means an easy transition, but I find myself beginning everything again and the temple has given me a fresh start and many new beginnings are looming. I have been particularly struck by the nembutsu practice, which I devotedly do every morning and I can't begin my day without that time with the Buddha. Pure Land Buddhism, and the experiences I have had, began to make sense to me when wading my way through a number of book study groups at the temple, both in person and on Zoom. I knew that I had found something special and that it just made sense to me. My fears of having to 'become a Buddhist' vanished! I love the peace, space and opportunity for solitude that has been available to me at the temple, to practice and have the freedom to form my own relationship to Pure Land Buddhism and to the Buddha. The Bright Earth community is a very friendly one. I am especially loving the chanting and discovering that the deeper I enter into that the more I can tap into inner peace, as well as Amida Buddha's love and light permeating all things and resting in knowing that I am accepted, just as I am. Namo Amida Bu.

Ethics as the door to awakening

Kaspa

Buddhism is full of precepts. There are hundreds of rules for monks and nuns, the five lay precepts, and many other lists of ideals from the six perfections to the eight fold path.

How do we relate to all of these ideals? At first glance sometimes they can appear like a list of rules and regulations to keep ourselves in line, but this is not the Buddhist approach.

Thinking of rules and regulations reminds me of the Christian tradition that I was part of as a child. I appreciate that there are many traditions of Christianity and that not all of them are like this – but there was something of 'be good or you're going to hell' in the way that I was taught.

I remember one line from a song from Sunday School, 'Envy, jealousy, malice, pride: they must never in your heart abide.' It wasn't spelled out what would happen if these were in your heart, but it was clear that it was something very bad. Whenever I was envious or jealous or malicious or proud I pretended that I wasn't and locked the feelings away deep in my unconscious mind. This 'be good or else' approach also supported the part of me that judged others, and I ended up looking down on people who weren't behaving as I thought they should be, which made it much more difficult for me to relate to others.

Even so, there was something inspiring about having an ideal way of behaving to aspire to, and sometimes that kept me on the straight and narrow. Precepts and vows can be inspiring and we'd be foolish to throw them away completely. So how else might we approach them?

In the most literal translation of the five lay precepts, they begin with the words, 'I undertake the training to....'

I like this attitude of training. It suggests an acceptance of our current state, as well as an acknowledgment that there is need for improvement. The idea of training is very different to the idea of 'follow these or else'. When you are a trainee you begin knowing very little and having little skill, and as you progress your knowledge and skills increase. We are always training in the precepts – moving towards the direction of understanding and following them, but never completely inhabiting them until we become buddhas ourselves, in some future lifetime.

In contrast to the view of religious vows I had as a child, from a Buddhist point of view, although there will be consequences to our actions, liberation is always possible. The Buddhist Wheel of Life illustrates all of the different realms one can be reborn into, from the realms of the gods to the human and animal realms to the various hells. If you look at a Wheel of Life closely you will see that in every realm there is a buddha, even in the hell realms where you can find demons boiling people in cauldrons of hot oil. Enlightenment is possible even from the worst of places, and even in the worst of places there will be a buddha loving you.

We can see that Buddhist precepts are an indication of what a buddha would do in this world. With this understanding we can use studying the precepts to deepen our experience of nembutsu. Studying the precepts brings us closer to the Buddha, and studying the actions we take in the world, often in contrast to the precepts, brings us closer to an understanding of our bombu nature. In this way the precepts become a container for our own awakening.

Every time we fail to keep a precept it is an opportunity for learning and for growing closer to the Buddha. When our faith in the Buddha is complete we follow the precepts naturally: we respond to whatever is in front of us with a loving heart. What stops our heart being full of faith is the fear that leads to greed, hate and delusion; fear of the unknown, fear of being out of control, fear of dukkha, and most existentially the fear of being separate and alone. When we act from fear we act selfishly, and we break the precepts.

If we think of the precepts in this way, whenever we notice that we are falling short, we can take it as an opportunity to investigate the specific failure of faith. What was the fear? When did it arise? We can also use this as an opportunity to bring ourselves closer to the Buddha, not only the act of simply remembering the Buddha, but allowing the Buddha to be kind and loving to whatever part of us is afraid. In this way our faith increases, and we are more likely to keep the precepts more closely in the future.

In a recent confirmation of ordination ceremony we began by reciting this Sange-mon verse from the Soto tradition of Zen Buddhism:

> I now entirely repent
> all the harmful actions I have perpetrated in the past,
> arising from beginningless greed, anger, and delusion,
> and manifested through body, speech, and mind.

Sange-mon is Japanese for "gate of contrition". This gate is into the field of awakening. Contrition is not guilt that we carry around with us like a stick we use to beat ourselves up with over and over again, but rather a genuine recognition of our faults and the harm we have caused. This real seeing of our human nature, both in the general case and in specific moments, may be accompanied by all sorts of feelings including guilt, anger and blame, but genuine contrition moves towards sadness, fellow-feeling and a recognition that we are loved even though we are a being that causes harm.

When we cause some harm in the world, to another person or to our environment, these actions and the way we treat them can get between us and the Buddha.

Daocho, who lived in the 6th and 7th Centuries, was a Chinese Buddhist master, a scholar of Pure Land Buddhism, a builder of many temples, and the teacher of Shandao. Towards the end of his life, he started to believe that he was not going to be born into the Pure Land. He felt weighed down with something, although he couldn't put his finger on what it was. There was something coming between him and the Buddha; something taking up the space where his faith had been.

One day he told his disciple Shandao about these feelings. That night Shandao had a dream about his teacher. The dream revealed that the karma weighing on Daocho was from all the insects and creatures that had been killed when Daocho was building temples. In the morning Shandao spoke to Daocho and suggested a public confession. Daocho realised that what his student was saying was true, and made an act of contrition in public. Supported by that ritual he was able to see his own nature clearly and to feel accepted by Amida Buddha just as he was. He felt once more that his rebirth in the Pure Land was assured.

The gift of working with the precepts is clear seeing, and clearly seeing our own nature is awakening itself.

If we act from ill-will or greed, and later can see ourselves clearly, we have the chance to bring the part that acted out into relationship to the Buddha. The more those parts of us are accepted and met with loving kindness, the less likely they are to act out again.

It can be difficult for us to accept that we have greedy and hateful parts of ourselves, or difficult to accept the consequences they lead to. Perhaps we are afraid of the feelings that will come up when we truly look at our own nature. Or perhaps we feel that if we really own those selfish impulses we will be rejected by those people we love, or the groups that we want to be a part of. In Pure Land Buddhism we are able to be contrite, to take an honest look at ourselves and to feel a tenderness towards our selfishness, because we trust that the Buddha is there feeling tender towards us.

Sometimes the Sangha can model this for us. The people that we practise with are able to accept and love us, even the parts of ourselves that we find difficult to love. Occasionally we act so wildly that the Sangha might struggle to love us, or at least they might take a while to get in touch with the love they have for us. This is why taking refuge in the Buddha is at the heart of our practice. Even the best human beings are not perfectly loving all of the time, but Amida can do this.

In our darkest moments we can always turn towards Amida and know that they love us just as we are. This is not just an abstract statement. Back in my first or second year of practising Pure Land Buddhism, on retreat out in rural France, I had a powerful experience of feeling held by the Buddha. I don't remember what, if anything, sparked it off. It wasn't in the shrine room, in fact I think I may have been alone, in one of the small animal houses that had been converted into monastic cell-like bedrooms. Perhaps I was thinking about some selfish act I had performed in the past, perhaps I had been primed by beginning to feel accepted by the community I was living in. I suddenly had a felt sense of the presence of the Buddha: something in the universe that could love me just as I was. I remember feeling profoundly undeserving and loved anyway. I saw myself in all my selfishness being loved by the Buddha, and it was unbelievable. It was a powerful and moving experience.

Not all experiences of contrition and of feeling close to the Buddha are as dramatic. Some people seem to get this kind of powerful experience when it's most helpful, in the early stages of their practice. Some people's experience is always quieter. I trust that we each get what we need. My experience of the Buddha these days is usually of a much softer background feeling, simply trusting in the love that is present in each moment.

In our practice sessions here at Bright Earth we recite the five lay precepts by asking for awareness of when we take life, take what is not freely given, and so on. In this way we are invited to release ourselves from judgement, and we enter into relationship with the precepts as a vehicle for awakening.

As Gyonen wrote, "The precepts are a jewelled boat to cross the river of desire. They are a divine carriage to traverse the mountain of hatred. They are an immediate cause of entering the citadel of awakening. They are a direct path leading to the realm of the buddhas. It is because of the precepts that the sustaining power of the Three Jewels, leading all beings to enlightenment, is forever fresh and new. The means of training thus provided for all kinds of beings has great saving virtue."[23]

Beth W's story

Beth loves being in nature, and is a therapist living in Worcester.

I first came to the temple several years ago as a supervisee receiving support and mentorship in my work with therapy clients. Visiting the temple so regularly was a gentle introduction to the idea of attending Buddhist practice there.

Parts of me struggle with self-doubt and feeling anxious. I have a part that grasps at being in control, and a part that gets into tangles in relationships. I remember first seeing the poem by Buddhist poet Zuigen Inagaki: 'Just as you are,' tears springing to my eyes as I felt a deep acceptance of ALL of me, probably for the first time in my life.

Pure Land Buddhism feels uncomplicated, a simplicity which makes it a form of Buddhism that feels accessible to me. There is a warmth and lightness with practice at Bright Earth; whether I attend regularly or drop in here and there, I feel just as welcome – more acceptance!

Being outdoors in green spaces, walking, pottering in my garden, all help to take me outside of myself and my internal noise. Being in nature brings me closer to Buddha and I find myself reciting the words: 'Namo Amida Bu' to express my gratitude and pure joy.

My faith in Buddha reminds me that I am loved and accepted just as I am. It is unwavering, and supports me to be more me, in my personal life and in my therapeutic relationships with clients. This faith helps me to practice self-compassion and compassion towards all living beings.

Despite having a small shrine at home, a more regular meditative practice of chanting nembutsu is a work in progress, as is attending regular practice at Bright Earth temple; I guess it is called 'practice' for good reason – I feel Buddha smiling!

Spiritual friendship

Satya

Shakyamuni Buddha's faithful assistant, Ananda, once said to him, 'Lord, I think that half of the Holy Life is spiritual friendship, association with the Lovely.' The Buddha replied: 'That's not so; say not so, Ananda. It is not half of the Holy Life, it is the whole of the Holy Life.'[24]

It is difficult for us to practise alone, or to live a spiritual life without any support. We are strongly affected by our conditions, and if all our friends eat meat or indulge in cruel gossip then it can be hard to be the odd one out. This is why it's important to see if we can find at least one or two friends who will support us on our path – who will encourage us to keep going and maybe gently challenge us when we lose our way.

Spiritual friendship and Sangha is also important because it's in relationship that we learn the most about ourselves. Ajahn Chah, a leading teacher in the Thai Forest Tradition, found that he could develop profound states of mind when he was meditating in the hills on his own, but that when he came back to live with the other monks he couldn't go for long without losing his patience with them and getting annoyed. After a few years he realised he had something to learn, and stayed in community more and more. He went on to develop his monasteries in this style. I have had the same experience after coming out of retreat feeling calm and slightly smug, and then spending a day with my family!

Looking for friends who support you on your own path doesn't mean finding people who are practising the same religion as you, or even people with any spiritual dimension to their lives. When you spend time in the company of particular friends, you will find yourself becoming a better version of yourself (or at least feeling inspired to be). These are the people who understand what it means to be human and who accept you as you are, but who also have faith in you and who cheer you on.

Colluding with others and having them collude with us is a comforting pastime, and sometimes it's just what we need for a little while, but the relief can be short-lived. Spiritual friends help us to face the sometimes harsh reality of life and of our own foolish nature head on, without losing heart. It is through facing these realities that we become open to grace.

For all these reasons we aspire in the Bright Earth Sangha to regularly come together and share Buddhist practice alongside our struggles, our vulnerabilities and our joys.

Practice

Nembutsu

Kaspa

Nembutsu is the practice of calling the name of Amida Buddha, or of saying the name of the Buddha in recognition that you have already heard his call. Nembutsu is an English transliteration of a Japanese word that is a translation of the Chinese word Nienfo. It is the practice we use to connect with something completely wise and loving that is outside the experience of our own small mind.

Buddhism suggests that there have been many buddhas, not just the historical Shakyamuni who lived and died in India and Nepal two and a half thousand years ago. The buddha we bring to mind when practising nembutsu is Amida Buddha, the Buddha of limitless light and life.

Shakyamuni Buddha told a story about Amida Buddha, saying that all beings who heard the name of Amida Buddha, with faith in their heart, would be reborn in Amida's Pure Land of love and bliss and from there become a fully enlightened being.

We can take this on its own terms – or think of it as a powerful myth that tells us something true and important about the nature of the universe and salvation.

In early Chinese Buddhism, the primary way of connecting to Amida Buddha was through visualisation practices. Nembutsu was bringing the Buddha to mind by creating an image of the Buddha in your mind's eye and then meditating upon that image. As well as visualisation practices there was also nembutsu recitation practice. In China they recited 'Namo Omito Fo'. Before the 7th century visualisation was seen as the most powerful way to invoke Amida. In the 7th century Shandao, a Chinese Buddhist master, realised that saying the name of Amida was enough to make a connection with that Buddha and guarantee rebirth in his Pure Land.

In mediaeval Japan there were various practices associated with Amida Buddha. These included recitation, but the idea that reciting Amida's name was sufficient for rebirth in the Pure Land had been lost until Honen rediscovered this idea through Shandao's writing. Honen went on to teach recitation of Amida's name as the unique and essential practice for rebirth in the Pure Land. Other practices were helpful and good for their own sake, he taught, but as foolish beings of wayward passion the only way to guarantee our enlightenment is to rely on the power of Amida Buddha. We can do this through reciting his name.

Shandao and Honen's understanding of practising verbal nembutsu initially came from reading the sutras and commentaries, but it was confirmed by their experience of doing the practice. I'm sure they both had a sense of being close to Amida and that they understood the nembutsu practice had created the conditions for this closeness. Honen had visions of Amida and the Pure Land throughout his life.

My own experience of reciting nembutsu is that it creates a container for our relationship to the Buddha, and that it keeps turning us back to Amida's light. We do not always see the light consciously, or have a felt sense of being close to the Buddha; sometimes our practice is clouded by frenetic thoughts or by greed, hate and delusion, but even in the midst of this we are being bathed in the light.

Whilst Honen emphasised practice, reciting the name daily and making special time for continuous nembutsu practice, Shinran, a disciple of Honen, emphasised faith, or the attitude of the practitioner. For Shinran the essential attitude was understanding that rebirth in the Pure Land, and thus enlightenment, was assured because Amida Buddha, a fully enlightened realised being of great power, was working on our behalf.

Honen rejected the 'buddha nature' argument, that all beings had the potential to become a buddha themselves, as in Japan at that time it was suggested that ordinary people couldn't realise their buddha nature, only ordained monks. Shinran re-imagined buddha nature as Amida's power working for each of us. We all have buddha nature, Shinran taught, in the sense that Amida is holding each of us in mind and will take us into his Pure Land. All we have to do is recognise that this is true and rebirth is assured. In this way of thinking, nembutsu becomes a rejoicing and a way of saying thank you for our guaranteed salvation, rather than a means to that salvation, and recitation is less important than remembering Amida's grace.

At Bright Earth we practise nembutsu with both of these attitudes; as a way of connecting with or tuning into Amida Buddha, and as a way of being grateful for our assured liberation by the Buddha's power.

As we say earlier there are many ways of understanding exactly what Amida is, but in some ways to ask if Amida Buddha is a real being sitting and practising in a land where the trees are made from precious gems (as their Pure Land is described) is to miss the most important point.

The promise of Amida Buddha that has been handed down to us points to a benign process at work in the universe. Not only are we acceptable to this benign process just as we are, but if we come into closer relationship with it, if we become participants in this process, our own liberation from dukkha is assured, and we become part of something bigger. Or — from a non-dual point of view — we simply need to remember that we are already part of this benign process.

This is what the nembutsu points to and aligns us to: the power of enlightenment working its way through the universe, liberating countless beings. As we invite this energy into our lives we become part of the dance of enlightenment.

If you come and practise with us, you will hear the nembutsu chanted in many different forms in our practice sessions, from the Sanskrit 'Amitabha', to the English gloss on the Japanese, 'Namo Amida Bu'. As well as hearing this chanted in practice, you will also hear 'Namo Amida Bu' spoken when people meet each other in the corridor, or when something goes wrong, or when something goes well.

Each time we recite the name of Amida we are reminding ourselves of the Buddha's promise to save all beings, and of the benign process of enlightenment at work in the world.

At home people recite nembutsu with a mala, or chant along to recordings of other's chanting, or simply say 'Namo Amida Bu' as they remember the Buddha throughout the day.

If you have your own mala you could make a practice of sitting and reciting 108 nembutsu each day, simply by saying 'Namo Amida Bu', or using one of the melodies we use when chanting nembutsu. Or you could download some of those chants and sing along with them for ten or twenty minutes a day.

Honen used to chant continually throughout the day, keeping it going in his own mind when he was chatting to people or just going about his business. He said that he would chant 60,000 nembutsu each day in this way. This kind of intense practice might be completely outside of your experience – but sometimes you might want to experiment with filling your mind with the Buddha throughout the whole day in this way.

Honen also encouraged his followers to make special times to put everything aside and just practise nembutsu for an extended period of time. We do this with our continuous chanting periods that Satya has written about. I find they are an invaluable way of deepening my own practice, and my experiences during those practice days remind me of the power of nembutsu.

Despite this practice, Honen also said that one nembutsu is enough, as it is Amida's power that liberates us. The extended periods of practice just help us to remember this.

Nembutsu is a way of keeping the Buddha in mind, and remembering that the saving grace of Amida is close to hand. Whatever brings us back to this knowledge can be a form of nembutsu, from a continuous recitation practice to simply having an image of the Buddha above our desk at work.

Namo Amida Bu.

Having a shrine

Satya

As human beings we often forget what is fundamentally important — loving each other, enjoying the present moment, doing what good we can with the time we have. We tend to get caught up in the minutiae of our lives, and tangled in our self-protective thoughts and feelings. Have I replied to that urgent email? What did he think about me when I said that? What will I cook for dinner?

Human beings are also powerfully conditioned by objects, and so one of the best ways of staying in relationship with something more fundamental than these everyday preoccupations is to surround ourselves with the right objects. We do this when we have pictures of our loved ones on our desk at work, art on our walls that inspires us, or houseplants that connect us to nature.

Buddhists often surround themselves with objects that represent the Buddha or Buddhist practice. We might use candles, incense or objects from nature. Our Buddha statues may be the big golden Thai Buddha on our main shrine which was given to the temple as a wonderful gift from our friend Caroline, or a cheap one made of plastic from a home furnishings store. All these objects can point us towards something in the universe that is infinitely wise and compassionate. This is what I aspire to be in relationship with, and conditioned by. This is where I have the best chance of the Buddha's qualities rubbing off on me as I experience myself in their field of merit.

A shrine is a further elaboration on bringing these good qualities into our homes. As we tend to them and spend time in front of them, spiritual associations build up and the shrine becomes more and more sacred. All rituals are designed to help us to deepen our connection with something – each other or particular phenomena – and the rituals we carry out around Buddhist objects help to strengthen our connection with the buddhas. Shrines can be places where we spend 'quality time' with the Buddha, maybe sitting quietly in meditation, or bowing in front of them twice a day, or asking the buddhas for help, or having a regular nembutsu practice.

How can you make yourself a Buddhist shrine? First get yourself a central statue, object or picture – something that you feel a connection with. I like to place Buddha rupas on my shrines. Some Pure Land Buddhists traditionally have a painting of the Japanese characters of the nembutsu as their central object. Find a good place for your shrine – the top of a bookcase, a shelf or a little table. I like to try and make shrines where they take a central position – not off in the corner of the room – but this will depend on your space. It's also good if possible to have space in front of the shrine where you can sit or bow.

You might want to find a cloth to place underneath the Buddha, to represent the ground, and if you like you could have a figure on either side of the Buddha to represent his attendants Quan Shi Yin and Tai Shih Chih (or the Pure Land ancestors Shandao and Honen).

When you approach your shrine do so in a respectful way, bowing to the Buddha. Make sure you keep your shrine clean and tidy. You might want to do your daily practice in front of your shrine, or offer incense once a day, or do three prostrations.

Something else that is nice to do is carrying a 'portable shrine' around with you when you go on holiday or travel – a small Buddha and a candle is enough, and maybe a mala. In this way you will be accompanied wherever you go.

Making offerings

Satya

Making offerings at the shrine is a way of showing respect to the Buddha, and of showing our gratitude for the three jewels. It's a bit like wanting your guest to eat your best food and stay in a room which has beautiful things in it.

There are a number of traditional offerings – fresh flowers in a vase, incense, food, something to represent music, water and candles or other lights. Some shrines have two bowls of water, representing water to drink and water to wash with. If you don't have an incense holder you can fill a small bowl with rice and use this to hold the burning incense.

Some Buddhist traditions have very precise rules for making offerings, but here at Bright Earth we think that the spirit of the offering is the most important thing. Arrange your offerings around the Buddha artfully, and maybe keep spare incense and a box of matches underneath the shrine. You might want to buy a singing bowl to ring before and after meditation too. When you don't have these things it is fine to improvise!

When you offer incense you can recite an offering verse, maybe eventually learning one or two off by heart. You can find these in Appendix E.

You can also make a water offering by pouring some water from a jug into two or three small bowls set in front of the Buddha, and then lifting these up high one by one. When you change the water make sure the blessed water goes into a plant pot or into the garden onto a living thing so that none of the blessings are lost.

How to write a Dharma Glimpse

Kaspa

What is a Dharma Glimpse?

A Dharma Glimpse is a short piece of writing, which demonstrates how the Dharma (or the truth) shows up in our ordinary lives. We experience something, and that experience brings insight, or compassion, or reminds us of a Buddhist teaching. A Dharma Glimpse is an expression of that moment. They can inspire others to see similar truths in their own lives, and they are a way of creating connection within our community.

Rev. Koyo Kubose, who led the Bright Dawn Center of Oneness Buddhism Lay Ministry programme for many years, introduced Dharma Glimpses to Satya and myself and we started using them in the Bright Earth temple in January 2022. We begin each of our practice sessions here with a Glimpse written by someone in our community. Here's how Rev. Koyo describes them:

"Question: What is the definition of a glimpse? Is it a spiritual connection, awareness, or coincidence that is realized, felt, or observed?

Answer: Yes, I can be all of these. In general, a glimpse is all about bringing the Buddhist teachings and insight into the everyday. The ideal glimpse is born out of some everyday activity that shines a light inward and relates to some dharma teaching, ideally something from our weekly reading. A glimpse can be about stars or cows or flat tires. They can be lyrical, serious, or funny, and the best is personal."

Writing Dharma Glimpses

Some people may be anxious about writing a Glimpse because they are worried about how other people might judge them. To those people we say, we'd love to read whatever you write. Some people may be wary of writing a Glimpse because they are not sure what a Glimpse is. Some people have already written Glimpses and we want to help them to refine their offerings.

Hopefully this guide will speak to all of these people. You don't need to read this whole guide in one go, or at all. Begin with the section that speaks to you.

"I'm not good enough"

It is very common for people to think they can't write Dharma Glimpses because they're 'not very good' at writing, because they don't know enough about Buddhist teachings, or because they feel self-conscious about what people might think as they read their Glimpses out in Buddhist practice.

Glimpses don't need to be written with perfect grammar or in poetic language. They don't need to be clever, or contain references to Buddhist scriptures. The best Glimpses are written by ordinary human beings! They are an opportunity to be honest about something that has gone wrong in your life, or to acknowledge a realisation you had (small or large) when going about your daily life. They are an opportunity to reflect on our human limitations, and to celebrate moments of wisdom and compassion. However little value you feel your Glimpse might have, try to trust that someone in the room will appreciate hearing it.

Three Top Tips

1) Begin very simply with one experience and one insight.

2) Take heed of Anne Lamott's advice to write a shitty first draft. Get something down on paper without worrying about how good it is. Then you have something to work from.

3) Perfect is the enemy of the good. When we aim for perfection, we can get so lost in worrying about that impossible target that we don't finish the piece. Or that we don't even start the piece. Better to have something on the page than nothing at all. Please have a go and send one to us, we'd love to read it.

Looking for Some Clear Guidelines?

A Dharma Glimpse is an account of an experience, and a recounting of the insight that came from that experience or the Buddhist teaching it reminded us of.

When writing Glimpses we try not to speak in generalisations, understanding that whilst there is something universal about spiritual experience, the way that spiritual experiences and insights show up in our lives is unique and is conditioned by our lives at that time.

Expressing a Dharma Glimpse in a personal and specific way allows the reader/listener to find their own relationship to our insight. We are not suggesting that our insight should be their insight, but giving them the space to find what resonates and makes sense in their own lived experience.

Dharma Glimpses may look and sound different to Dharma teachings that Buddhist teachers give or write. Buddhist teachers speak from many years of experience and are authorised to teach by their communities. With a Dharma Glimpse we are sharing our experience rather than giving a teaching.

Practical Tips for Writing

Ask: "What is the experience?" & "What is the fresh insight, learning or moment of being moved to compassion?"

When you are first writing Glimpses, think of them as a game of two halves. Begin by writing about the moment in your life, and finish by writing what you have learnt.

For Glimpses that we read out in our Buddhist practice sessions:

• Aim to have one insight per glimpse
• Aim to write no more than one side of A4

We check all Glimpses that are going to be read in practice sessions and may occasionally offer feedback or ask for changes to be made. When Glimpses are read out at practice sessions they are representing the Bright Earth community and so we need to make sure that, for example, the Glimpse doesn't include discriminatory language.

Glimpses and Journaling

Journaling is an important and useful spiritual practice. In a journaling practice we might write about questions we are working through, and life issues we are struggling with. We might write a letter to the Buddha, or do some parts work using Internal Family Systems. These are all good things to do but they are not necessarily Dharma Glimpses.

A Dharma Glimpse is usually written following the insight and is a written expression of what we have learnt. However, we might choose to share a piece of writing that is more like a piece of journaling in the spirit of sharing our process. A Glimpse like this is less about a particular insight and more an appreciation of the journey we are on.

Beginning with Not Knowing

Sometimes we might begin writing a Glimpse without knowing what the insight is. As you are writing you discover the insight. If you are writing in this way, once you have finished the first draft and realised what the insight is you might choose to go back and edit the whole thing, taking out anything that confuses your central point.

Breaking the Rules

If the rule for a Dharma Glimpse is to write about an experience, and then write about what you learnt from that, then we can also imagine Glimpses that break those rules, but still have the feel of a Glimpse.

For example, a sonnet is defined as a fourteen line poem, written in iambic pentameter with a specific rhyme scheme. Shakespeare's sonnets ended with a couplet that usually expressed the conclusion of the poem, or invited us to see the previous quatrains in a new light.

When modern poets write sonnets they often break one or two of these rules. They might write fourteen lines of blank verse without using iambic pentameter, but keep the final two lines as a conclusion or turning point of the poem. Even though this doesn't follow all the rules we know this is still a sonnet because it looks more or less the same and most importantly has the same feel.

In the same way we can keep what is essential about a Dharma Glimpse without using the exact form of: experience + insight.

Maybe our Dharma Glimpse is an image, or a song or a poem. Maybe it's a piece of prose where the insight comes before the experience, or they are interwoven through the piece.

It's possible to keep the spirit of a Glimpse and go beyond the basic form. If it comes from your lived experience, is expressed in a personal way and expresses a moment of learning or being moved then we can still recognise it as a Dharma Glimpse.

Beginning with a Buddhist Teaching

Not sure what to write about? Turn the Dharma Glimpse upside down. Pick a Buddhist principle or teaching and then ask what it reminds you of in your own life.

For example, when I think of impermanence I think of the clock in my office that has just broken. Things breaking. Time passing. I could write a Dharma Glimpse about that.

Or, when I think of the four noble truths, I suddenly remember a moment in the week when I suffered, had an emotional reaction but then was able to pause before acting out... That's another Dharma Glimpse.

Or, when I think of Shinran saying, "If good people go to the Pure Land how much more true for evil people," I remember seeing someone I don't like receiving kindness and that's another Glimpse...

Regular Practice

Our suggestion is that you keep notes of possible Dharma Glimpses, and commit to writing one once a month or once a fortnight. Try this for a while as a personal practice and see if it helps you to find more Dharma around you. You are welcome to send them to us or not.

In Conclusion

Hopefully this guide has reassured you, if that's what you needed, or offered you more guidance if that's what you were looking for. Hopefully you feel more confident about writing a Dharma Glimpse now. Remember, someone will appreciate what you write.

Bowing and prostrations

Satya

When I first attended Buddhist practice in the Buddhist House in Narborough, the bit that made me the most uncomfortable was when everyone made a semi-circle around the Buddha and, after kneeling, dropped forward to put their foreheads on the carpet. I copied them as they lifted their forearms above their heads, palms up. My face was burning with self-conscious embarrassment, and I wanted to bolt from the room.

When I moved to Malvern with Kaspa and we started running Buddhist practice in our tiny living room (which looked out onto the street), I remember feeling embarrassed that passers-by might look in and see us prostrating. Even the word 'prostrate' left me feeling unsettled. It either reminded me of prostate cancer or conjured a kind of naked helplessness I didn't want to dwell on.

Bowing can be particularly challenging for Westerners. Our culture tells us that we should be self-sufficient, and that we shouldn't put ourselves below anyone else where we will be vulnerable. Judith Lief says,

> "As Westerners we tend to think of prostrating as a gesture of defeat or abasement. We think that to show someone else respect is to make ourselves less. Prostrating irritates our sense of democracy, that everyone is equal....
>
> On one hand we want to receive the teachings but on the other we don't really want to bow down to anyone or anything."[25]

Of course, a feeling of naked helplessness is one of the points of prostrations. When we lie flat on our bellies in front of the Buddha we are exposing the back of our necks, which was a traditional way of showing strangers that we trusted them. If they wanted to, they could easily ambush us with their sword.

I have to make an effort now to remember how it felt to do prostrations back then, as prostrations are one of my favourite practices now. There is something about resting my forehead on the ground that is a great relief – I can let go of all my self-protective energy and my efforts to be in control, and relax on the ground with the Buddha watching over me. Sometimes when I am doing prostrations alone I will linger on the floor, not wanting to get up, feeling the muscles in my back relaxing bit by bit.

Bowing and prostrations can be found in all the world's religious traditions, and the practice has a variety of different functions or effects. We bow to each other as a social courtesy, or as a form of repentance. We prostrate to deities to establish a worshipful relationship with them, or to say thank you to them. We bow to increase our humility and to decrease our self-protective ego. We bow because we belong on the floor. We let ourselves down onto the floor and we feel Mother Earth supporting us.

Bowing and full prostrations are used in various ways in Pure Land Buddhism. Here at Bright Earth we do a set of three full prostrations at the end of practice – the first prostration to the Buddha, then the Dharma and the Sangha. We also bow a lot both during formal practice and elsewhere – if in doubt, bow! During formal practice we bow to our seats in the shrine room to show respect, we bow to ask permission to enter the sacred space around the shrine, we bow to each other, we bow to the room when we enter or exit, we bow after meditating or to the celebrant to say thank you for the Dharma talk. In less formal situations, we bow after we bless the food, to visitors when we greet them, or to each other. I like to bow to our big Buddha in the garden alcove whenever I pass him (although if I bowed to every Buddha in the temple when I walked past I'd never get anywhere very quickly!).

A bow is a bit like saying the nembutsu – it puts us into relationship with the buddhas, and it reminds us of our position in relation to the infinite – how small and limited we are, and how grateful we can be for all the things we receive.

Try one out right now. Put your hands together in the gassho (Japanese) mudra (also known as the anjali mudra in Sanskrit), as if you are praying, with your hands upright and palms together at chest level. Bow at the waist – bow as if you mean it. I am bowing back.

Breathing nembutsu

Satya

One of the advantages of the breathing nembutsu practice is that you can do it anywhere – on a busy train, sitting in your living room while other people are watching television, or in the middle of the night when you wake up and feel suddenly frightened by life or by death.

To do the practice you imagine the words of the nembutsu accompanying your breath as it naturally rises and falls. During the in-breath you imagine the syllables 'Namo A–' and during the out-breath you imagine '–mida Bu'. You could also use 'Ami–' and 'tabha'. Don't try to alter the length of your breath – some breaths will be short or shallow, some will be longer. Just allow the nembutsu to follow your breath as a cork would bob up and down on gentle waves.

As you continue, see if you can allow the nembutsu to become more and more fluid. There may be a natural pause on the first 'a' of Amida as your breath pauses between coming in and going out again. There will also be a complete break after the 'Bu' as your body pauses before taking in another breath. Allow these pauses to be there.

Sometimes the nembutsu I imagine accompanying my breath has a tune – the tune of the chant we use for our prostrations. Sometimes it doesn't. Sometimes I imagine a golden glow accompanying the chant, or the presence of Amida Buddha. You can experiment and see what feels right for you. It doesn't matter too much though. As with all Pure Land practice we're not looking for 'results' like feeling calmer or feeling more connected to the Buddha (although these will often be happy by-products). We are simply bringing ourselves into relationship with something bigger than ourselves. We can trust that this will be a helpful thing to do in the long run. We can also trust that we have already been "grasped, never to be abandoned" by Amida (the quote is by Shinran) and that our nembutsu are a flowering of our gratitude.

The breathing nembutsu also works well if you are doing a period of quiet sitting. Sit upright in your usual meditation posture on a meditation cushion or on a chair and allow the nembutsu to follow your breath. When you get distracted (you will!) simply bring your attention back to the nembutsu. You could set yourself a timer on your phone and do five or fifteen minutes, or simply sit for as long as you feel is good for you to sit.

Continuous nembutsu

Satya

One of my favourite Pure Land practices is the continuous nembutsu. During continuous nembutsu, the chant carries on in the shrine room for the duration of the practice. Most often we do two hours but for special occasions it's quite special to do longer – six or even twenty four hours.

We have developed our own way of doing continuous nembutsu here at Bright Earth, which is different from the way it is traditionally done in Japanese temples (where the chant is often a monotone). We use a simple chant and tune written by our minister colleague Kusuma: 'Namo Amida Buu-Tsu, Namo Amida Buu-uu-Tsu'. We alternate between sitting and walking, and the nembutsu is accompanied by the mokugyo, a wooden drum. The mokugyo keeps us in time and it adds some percussion to the chanting.

We sit for twenty minutes, walk slowly around the shrine for twenty minutes (still chanting), sit for twenty minutes and so on. The chant begins on one note, but as time goes on little slides up and down are introduced and become exaggerated – by the end of the first hour we are usually chanting with several harmonies. Sometimes the chant is in a minor key and sometimes major, sometimes it is lively and sometimes elegiac, sometimes it is tuneful and sometimes not!

As the day progresses, different people appear and join in the walking or sitting. Others leave to have a cup of tea, or to eat in the room next door before they re-enter the shrine room. It's lovely to see old friends appearing at the door – some who've travelled quite some way to join in, and to hear their familiar voices blending with the others. It's also lovely to see new faces – people who've never been to the temple before – and to see them gradually relax into the practice.

Chanting in this way can be a challenging practice for some people to begin with. Chanting isn't something most of us are used to doing in the UK, and people sometimes feel self-conscious at the sound of their own voice and worried about getting it 'wrong'. Combine this with the unfamiliar etiquette of the shrine room and people can feel very outside of their comfort zone. Generally if they stay long enough they relax into the chanting and forget about what other people might be thinking of them. As their voices grow a little louder and they remember to bow when the bell rings, they blend into the group and it can feel like we know them without having shared a single word with them (or rather, having shared three words over and over again!).

The continuous nembutsu practice has a knack of showing you yourself like a very wise mirror. One of the things I used to struggle with a lot was not being in control of what happens in the room. When you are on your own, or when you are leading practice, you can change the pitch or speed of the chant at will. When there are five or ten of you, you can try and speed things up or slow things down, but if the room doesn't want to do that, they won't obey! The chant really does take on a life of its own, and after many sessions of continuous nembutsu I am beginning to get the message. I notice anxiety coming up when things aren't going how I think they should be going (maybe the chant is out of tune or a new person doesn't seem to be relaxing into it). I notice the impulse to try and 'make it better' – chanting more loudly so others are forced into copying me, or smiling too much at the new person. I return to the chanting and feel the anxiety gradually ebbing away. Sometimes this pattern is repeated many times before I finally surrender to the group, stop worrying about others, and put my focus back onto the chanting and the Buddha where it belongs.

Different people experience different things during the chanting. Some feel annoyed by the sound of someone's regular coughing, or feel driven to distraction by how fidgety they feel when we sit for twenty minutes. Others think it all seems a bit silly. We are all unique and we all see ourselves reflected back in unique ways in the mirror of the chanting. We can learn a lot about ourselves on these days, sometimes things we'd rather not have known.

The chanting has a very different effect on different people. Some people find that, within the container of the nembutsu and the people present, difficult emotions bubble up and spill over. One new member, who was an experienced Buddhist practitioner in a different school, said that he was surprised about how emotional he found the experience, and that as he chanted sadness rose up from nowhere. Someone else reported remembering painful childhood memories, and found it difficult to stay in the shrine room for a while. Sometimes people feel spaced out with bliss or deeply calm, sometimes they feel a bit embarrassed, and sometimes they feel nothing at all.

I often find the experience of chanting quite mundane – I think about having a cup of tea in ten minutes, or some job I have to do tomorrow, or my mind just goes blank. As the years have gone on, I do feel more joy during the chanting, and feel more settled in it – the time seems to whoosh by in a way that it rarely did when I first attended the practice and five minutes could last forever. It's often towards the end of the day or later that the effects of the practice catch up with me. I find myself being overwhelmed with gratitude at someone new arriving, or by looking at the smile on the Buddha's face. Tears often come at this point and I have to stop chanting until my voice stops catching. I also feel an 'after-effect' of the chanting over the next days and weeks – I feel more stable, more grounded, and more in touch with the beauty of the world.

Once when we were chanting in a beautiful Quaker meeting house, Howard (who was struggling with his health) lay down on some cushions at the back where he chanted or just listened. As I walked around I remember feeling great gratitude for the fact that he was resting for me, and that I was keeping on walking and chanting for him. It was as if we had become one person and so it was possible for me to both rest and to chant – I didn't have to do it all. This is Sangha as refuge.

After such long periods of hearing the same phrase over and over, the chant can stay with you. After one eleven hour chanting session I lay in bed that night and listened to a choir quietly singing Namo Amida Bu in my head. It wasn't that I was imagining it – I could hear the voices as if they were outside of me. You could make sense of this as some of my brain cells getting stuck on a loop, or you could see it as a spiritual experience. It doesn't matter – either way it was a lovely thing to listen to as I went to sleep.

Continuous chanting is special as it gives us a more immersive experience of chanting and of hearing the nembutsu. It brings us together with others from our Sangha, and it shows us how we are bombu beings in relationship with Amida Buddha. We're not in control of very much – all we can do is say the name of Amida and trust that we will be looked after. Continuous chanting shows us that we can trust – the chant goes faster or slower depending on what the group needs, and people show up with delicious food to keep us nourished and with smiles or a wink to revive us when we need reviving at three o'clock in the afternoon when we're feeling sleepy and bored.

We let go into the group and we know that we will be held – by each other, by the sacred space, and by the golden Buddha, who watches us for hour after hour and who is delighted that we are there with them.

Listening circle

Satya

One of the sacred spaces we create here at Bright Earth is the listening circle. What follows is a list of instructions and suggestions if you'd like to hold your own listening circle.

When holding listening circles it is, if possible, helpful to have at least one person present who has had experience of this kind of sharing before and who feels comfortable holding the space and modelling both listening and sharing from the heart. The more experienced people there are present, the more grounded the space will feel. If there are more newer or nervous people present, the group will usually unconsciously limit the depth of their sharing. People tend to share at the edges of what feels possible for them, and sometimes this might be a few sentences about the weather or their day. As you continue to meet, and as faith grows, you may find people sharing their emotions more often, or being more vulnerable. This can't be rushed!

It may occasionally be necessary to hold a boundary. In the listening circle the boundaries will be both explicit and implicit, and delineate the specific culture that makes the space safer than most spaces. These explicit and implicit rules might include starting and finishing on time, people turning off their phones, having timed shares, everyone listening carefully to each other, and the use of a room where the group won't be interrupted. An example of a boundary breach is if someone starts speaking when someone else is holding the stone. It is important for those speaking to know that they can speak without anyone else responding. If others interrupt and they're not gently corrected, it potentially leaves the whole group feeling unsure about whether or not this will happen to them as well. The facilitator can find a way of gently holding boundaries – maybe by waiting until the speaker has finished, or maybe holding up their hand and asking the speaker if they're willing to pause whilst they say something like, "a reminder that this group works differently to most spaces and so we are all quiet whilst someone else is speaking – this is so we can all be listened to properly and also feel safe to speak without having others comment on what they're saying. We're all learning as we go and so don't worry about getting things wrong – I'll let people know about the boundaries like this when I need to as we go along. Thank you all – speaker – please do continue."

If the group is more experienced, group members may share their thoughts and feelings about other people who are present in the group – e.g. if they have appreciated something they shared earlier, or if they have had a difficult interaction elsewhere which is unresolved. They might choose to give the stone to the person they've shared about, who can then hold the stone and respond to what's been said, and the stone can be 'swapped back and forth' a few times until the issue has been resolved (or at least aired). This does take the group into different territory and so we'd advise that you only do this with groups of experienced sharers.

If you have new people attending the circle (as we do here at the temple) it may be helpful to read some guidelines out at the beginning of the hour. I have copied ours below which you might want to use or adapt.

Once the allocated time is up, or if everyone has said what they want to say and there is a period of silence when no-one picks up the stone again, we like to finish with five minutes of the nembutsu and then the closing verse. We finish by bowing to each other in gratitude for each other's presence, and then to the Buddha.

You might want to hold listening circles as part of a retreat day (they fit well at the beginning, and/or at the end so people can reflect on their experience of the day), after practice or on its own. They can easily be held online, e.g. on Zoom. Remind people that listening is the most important part, remember that the circle is held by Amida, and enjoy the deepening of truth, connection and faith that this practice will bring.

Listening circle guidelines

To be read out at the start of each meeting.

- We finish at 7.30pm or earlier.
- Please keep everything you hear confidential.
- When someone has the stone, everyone else is quiet and listens.
- When you are handed the stone, introduce yourself and then say what is in your heart. You can be quiet if you prefer.
- We don't give advice – instead we learn by listening to others speaking from their own experience.
- If others do speak of a theme that inspires you, you can speak of the theme as it relates to you rather than repeating what they've said.
- If it is a big group, please be conscious of how long you speak for (or you can do timed shares using a phone with an alarm – the advantage of this is that people don't have to worry about how long they're speaking for).
- When you are finished speaking, put the stone back in the middle.
- Feel free to attend every week or every so often. Do bring others – all are welcome. (You might also mention donations.)

A simple daily practice

Satya

Why start a daily practice?

If you are interested in exploring the Buddha's teachings, we recommend starting a daily practice at home, even if you can only spare a few minutes a day. Practice helps us to integrate Buddhist teachings into our everyday lives. It reminds us that we can take refuge in something reliable. It helps us to get to know ourselves. Over time, we may notice ourselves becoming more kind, more patient and more peaceful. There is no substitute for spiritual practice – we can read and discuss thousands of books without being transformed in the way that practice transforms us. Practice affects us in mysterious ways...

What is Bright Earth's approach to practice?

We are a Mahayana school of Buddhism and we are heavily influenced by Pure Land Buddhism. As you will know by now the practice for Pure Land Buddhists is simply saying the nembutsu, the name of Amida Buddha. We usually use the form 'Namo Amida Bu' which is derived from the Japanese. There are various tunes and you can either count your nembutsu, using a mala (like a Buddhist rosary) or not. We have a free 30-day email course on our website if you'd like to give nembutsu a try.

During our practice sessions here at Bright Earth temple we also do silent sitting, listen to Dharma Glimpses from members of our community, listen to Dharma talks, make bows to the Buddha and do walking meditation in the temple garden. All of these forms of Buddhist practice and others can be helpful.

Here at Bright Earth we also have an emphasis on ecological Buddhism that connects us with the Earth and that encourages us to take care of the Earth and all living beings. Some of our practice takes place outside – for example walking meditation on the hills. We also encourage engaged Buddhism, e.g. silent vigils for the Earth in our local town, and everyday Buddhism, e.g. incorporating practice into your day by saying grace before eating or bowing to the Buddha in your hallway when you pass.

Where and when should I do my practice?

Rev. Koyo Kubose of Bright Dawn recommended having a Special Place Of Tranquility (SPOT) where you can do your daily practice. This might be a corner of a bedroom, a quiet space in the spare room or a particular spot in the garden. You could make a small shrine with a buddha statue or an image of a buddha in the centre. You can add a candle, incense, flowers, or any other special objects.

When you do your practice will depend on your schedule and how busy the rest of your life is. Some people find it helpful to set their alarm a little early and do their nembutsu practice before the tasks of their day begin. Some people do a little walking meditation in their lunch break or put time aside before dinner or before they go to bed. Experiment and see what works for you.

What should I actually do for my daily practice?

Daily practice in the Bright Earth tradition is a very personal thing (in other Buddhist traditions it may be more prescribed). We would encourage you to choose from a 'menu' of different practices, decide how much time you can spare, and try it out – making adjustments as you go. Here are some elements you could choose from:

- You could incorporate two gasshos (bows) into your practice using Rev. Koyo Kubose's 'Everyday Gassho'[26] – in brief, bow to the Buddha once in the morning, saying 'harmony', and once in the evening, saying 'gratitude'.

- You could do five or ten minutes of nembutsu chanting, with or without a mala (a string of beads to help you count your recitations).
- Do some chanting to other buddhas or bodhisattvas – there are some chants on our website or find them on YouTube or elsewhere.
- You could do some silent sitting – just sit quietly and pay attention to your breath or do some breathing nembutsu.
- You could make an offering to the Buddha on your shrine, lighting a stick of incense or making an offering of flowers or water.
- You could make some bows or full prostrations to the Buddha.
- You could go for five minute of slow, silent walking around your garden or your local park, or sit quietly outside somewhere.
- You could start or finish your practice by reciting the refuges and the precepts, or reciting our closing verse – all in our Appendices.

We would suggest that you keep it simple to start with, and make it short enough to be manageable daily or almost daily. Alongside this short period of 'formal' practice, you might want to incorporate reminders of the Buddha into your daily life with the informal practice suggestions below:

- Learn a blessing and say it before meals as a way of reminding yourself to be grateful for the food you receive.
- Say 'Namo Amida Bu' or 'Namo Amitabha' out loud or silently during the day when you remember to.
- Whenever you pass your shrine, bow to the Buddha.
- Carry a mala with you and use them to recite nembutsu.
- Pause when going in or out of doors to take a centring breath (one slow breath that reconnects you to yourself and to the ground underneath you).
- Remember the Buddha when walking in nature or at difficult moments.

- Pause for a minute between appointments and remember the Buddha.
- Remember to be grateful.

How do I know if I'm 'doing it right'?

You may not feel more peaceful after your practice, or think that you are receiving any benefits at all. Persevere, and pay attention to how your daily life is feeling. Buddhist practice works on us all differently, and we can trust that it is helpful to do.

Practice as gratitude

Many Pure Land Buddhist teachers say that it isn't necessary to do any Buddhist practice in order to become enlightened. Simply saying the nembutsu ensures that we are accepted by Amida Buddha just as we are now, and it also that we will go to the Pure Land (the field of merit that surrounds Amida Buddha) when we die.

This means that rather than something we need to do in order to be accepted or in order to 'improve ourselves', Buddhist practice is seen as an expression of gratitude for what we have already received. You might want to experiment with this approach as you practice. How would it be to trust that you have already been 'grasped, never to be abandoned' (Shinran) by Amida Buddha? What if you really were acceptable just as you are?

Do feel free to take what you like and leave the rest. If any of these ideas don't feel right to you at the moment, that's fine. Choose whatever is comfortable, keep an open mind, and continue to practise. As Rev. Koyo Kubose would say, keep going!

Enjoy your daily practice. Namo Amida Bu.

Bright Earth Buddhist practice and ceremonies

Satya

Here at the temple in Malvern we run Buddhist practice for members of the public twice a week. This has changed over time and may continue to change, but to give you a taste here is what we currently do. You are very welcome to join these practice sessions live on Zoom or later by visiting our YouTube channel: www.youtube.com/brightearth

Our big gong in the hallway is rung five minutes before the start of practice, to symbolically summon people to practice. People enter the shrine room and sit quietly on chairs or cushions on the floor until practice begins.

The celebrant (whoever is leading the practice for that day) enters and the bellperson rings a large bell to signify the start of practice. Everyone bows.

We begin with a Dharma Glimpse, written by a member of our community and read out by another member of our community. We try to include different people in practice — reading glimpses, reading the incense offering verse, learning how to do the role of bellperson — we learn different things from taking part in different ways.

Next the celebrant leads us in a period of silence, with some chanting after ten minutes or so, followed by some more silence. We often chant 'Amitabha' but there are many different chants we use to different buddhas and bodhisattvas – some of these can be found on our website.

After a bell to finish the silent sitting, the celebrant leads us in repeating the three refuges, the five precepts, the three active virtues and the Bodhisattva vows. You can find these in our liturgy section in the Appendices of this book or online.

The celebrant then gives a short Dharma talk about a Buddhist teaching or about something that has happened during the week.

We finish by making three prostrations to the main shrine, accompanied by the 'Namo Amida Bu' chant. The celebrant makes an incense offering, we return to our places, and finish by bowing to each other and the Buddha and then reciting the closing verse together:

Blessed by Amitabha's light
May we care for all living things
and the holy Earth

During practice we all take care to show our respect to the Buddha, the shrine room and each other. For example, when someone comes in at the beginning and sits opposite us we bow to them, and we bow to our seat at the end of practice to thank it for supporting us.

We tune into each other by taking our lead from the celebrant, and we try to move more quietly and gracefully than we might elsewhere. The atmosphere that builds is one of reverence and quiet contemplation, often punctured by lighter moments when the celebrant laughs at themselves for making a mistake, or makes jokes during their Dharma talk.

There are various advantages to following a more formalised structure when practising together. One is that it joins the Sangha together – we are all doing the same thing at the same time, and we repeat this over and over. Becoming familiar with the various elements of practice engraves the nembutsu more deeply into our hearts, like repeated readings of a favourite poem. A more formal mode of practice can also remind us (or help newcomers to discover) how important it is that we put the Buddha at the centre of our lives.

My own experience of attending practice regularly is that, regardless of how I feel at the start, it is often a doorway into gratitude, peace, and a tangible feeling of being closer to the Buddha. This isn't always the case – sometimes I spend Saturday morning practice wishing I'd eaten some breakfast first, or wondering if the sitting meditation will ever end. Practice isn't a shortcut to bliss, or a method by which we become perfect human beings. As we bring ourselves into relationship with the Buddha, however, their qualities really do start rubbing off on us – bit by bit.

Practice is often the place where I receive insights about myself and others, either in meditation or whilst chanting, or whilst listening to the Dharma talk. It is also the place where I tend to have spiritual experiences: sudden whooshes of gratitude, fellow feeling and intimacy with all things that bring me to tears. These might happen as I watch a blackbird balancing on the railing outside the big window behind the Buddha, or as I listen to us all as we chant Amida's name. Practice is where Quan Yin Bodhisattva visits me, and where I am able to peel off thin layers of ego one by one and discard them on the floor behind me. Practice is where the light gets in.

Here at the temple we follow our practice sessions with a cup of tea in the dining room which is next door to the shrine room. This gives people a chance to get to know each other and to ask any questions they might have about practice, or about Buddhism in general.

A couple of times a month we follow this cup of tea with an hour's work – 'mindful maintenance' – cleaning the house or working in the temple garden. There is always plenty to be done... Working together is a crucial part of Sangha building. As Buddhists we are learning how to be of service to our Sangha and local community and ultimately to all sentient beings. We can start by washing up some mugs!

Regardless of how different Bright Earth groups run their practice sessions, the important thing is that we are gathering together to say the name of Amida Buddha, and sharing this practice with each other. We turn up as we are, with our current preoccupations and anxieties, and with all our self-protection and our self-doubt. As we practise we hand all this over to the Buddha and trust that the nembutsu is working on us, often despite our unconscious attempts to push it away and to cling onto our self-protection. Little by little, we are transformed under the loving gaze of the Buddha. We let go of our fear. We become buddhas practising with other buddhas. We luxuriate in this love. And then we take this love out into our daily lives and we offer it to others.

Appendices

Appendix A: Our assumptions

Kaspa & Satya

It is impossible to perfectly describe our beliefs about how the Universe works, partly because words are always inadequate in the face of such vast mysteries, and partly because we will continue to learn from our experiences and make revisions. As provisional and incomplete as they are, we still feel that it is helpful to share the assumptions on which Bright Earth's spirituality rests. We understand that:

- There is a source of infinite love and wisdom that is always present and that accepts us just as we are.
- This love is inside us, outside us, and moves through us. It is not always easy to see.
- A good life is lived in awareness of this love and guided by this love.
- One way of seeing this love is as the light of Amida Buddha, whose name means limitless light and life.
- Human beings all contain this light at their centres. This is often covered up by layers of protection that show up as greed, ill will and delusion.
- These protective layers relax and melt away under the light of the Buddha's love.
- Getting to know our own particular ways of staying safe and being compassionate to these protective parts of ourselves can also help them to relax.

- When our protective parts relax we are more able to feel our connection to the Buddha, and to all life.
- People who continue to live in this light tend to become more relaxed, more compassionate to all beings and more full of joy.

Appendix B: How to connect with the Bright Earth community

Satya

At the time of writing, the main Bright Earth community is clustered around the temple in Great Malvern where Kaspa & I live with seven templemates, three dogs and a cat. We open the temple for practice twice a week as well as offering retreat days, meditation classes, kirtans, mindful walks and more.

As our ministry training continues we hope to have more offerings available both online and hopefully face to face in different parts of the UK and the world.

On our website you'll find details of how to join our Buddhist practice, book groups and more either online or by coming to the temple – www.brightearth.org.

We also have a free email course on starting a daily nembutsu practice, recorded chants and more.

Our newsletter is at brightearth.substack.com.

Do feel free to email kaspa@kaspathompson.co.uk or satya@satyarobyn.com if you have any questions about anything you've read in this book or if you'd like to make contact.

Appendix C: Bright Earth liturgy

Refuges

Trad. & K. Thompson & S. Robyn
(repeat after the celebrant)

For refuge I go to the Buddha
The one who is awake and full of love
Namo Buddhaya
For refuge I go to the Dharma
All that guides us to wisdom and compassion
Namo Dharmaya
For refuge I go to the Sangha
Those who live in the Buddha's light
Namo Sanghaya

Precepts

Trad. & D. Brazier
(repeat after the celebrant)

With faith in the three jewels
and in light of my human tendencies
I pray that I may become aware
of when I take life
I pray that I may become aware
of when I take what is not freely given
I pray that I may become aware
of when I fall into sexual misconduct
I pray that I may become aware

of when I fall into wrong speech
I pray that I may become aware
of when I become intoxicated

Three Active Virtues
Terrance Keenan
(repeat after the celebrant)
No blame / Be kind / Love everything

Bodhisattva Vows
Genshin
(call and response)
Innumerable are sentient beings
We vow to save them all
Inexhaustible are deluded passions
We vow to transform them all
Immeasurable are the Dharma teachings
We vow to master them all
Infinite is the Buddha's way
We vow to fulfil it completely

Closing verse
Blessed by Amitabha's light
May we care for all living things
and the holy Earth

Dawn Prayers

Verse on Impermanence (by Shandao, following the Avatamsaka)

Time has passed with the swiftness of light;
It is already morning
Impermanence rushes upon us every moment;
Mara follows every step.
Oh, practitioners of the Way,
Strive diligently!
Attain Nirvana!

Resolution (Shandao following the Majjhima Nikaya)

Rare is it to meet with the Dharma, ultimate and profound,
Even though one seeks for hundreds and thousands of aeons
Fortunately we now hear and receive it
We pray that we may understand the Tathagata's true meaning
Let the Blessed One teach the Dharma,
let the Sublime One teach the Dharma
There are beings with little dust in their eyes
who are wasting through not hearing the Dharma
There will be those who will understand.
The Buddha has said:
Open for them are the doors of the deathless
Let those with ears now show their faith.

Refuges & Invocation (Brazier, following Shandao)

Buddhas throughout space and time, reverently do we adore you.
Dharmas to the end of time, reverently do we adore you.
Sanghas so exemplary, reverently do we adore you.
To this holy place, Amida Buddha, Highest One, bring your presence now
I pray
To this holy place, Shakyamuni, Enlightened One, bring your presence
now I pray
To this holy place, Tathagatas of all worlds, bring your
presence now I pray

Appendix D: Ancestor Prayer

We pause to remember our ancestors.

We remember our Indian ancestors, firstly Shakyamuni who was born in Lumbini and enlightened in Bodhgaya and set the dharma wheel turning in this age.

We remember those who came before Shakyamuni and passed their wisdom to him.

We remember Mahapajapati who walked one hundred and fifty miles one step after another before becoming the first Buddhist nun.

We remember the monastic and lay disciples of the Buddha, and generations of teachers that spread Buddhism through the East and throughout the world and who refreshed the precious dharma.

We remember awakened beings of all spiritual traditions trusting that wisdom appears in the world in many different ways, at many different times, in many different places.

We call to mind the wisdom of marginalised and oppressed groups, much of which has already been lost.

We remember our biological ancestors, our parents and grandparents, known and unknown, generations stretching back through time to the first humans in Africa.

We remember the ancestors of our chosen families.

We remember the ancestors of our own mindstream, the beings of our previous lives who practised dharma and brought light and joy to others.

We remember people across the world who stood against oppression and for human rights and the rights of all living things and for the earth.

We remember those who have oppressed and marginalised and harmed.

We carry the legacies of all of these ancestors, their gifts and their burdens. How wonderful to have the opportunity to work with all that has been handed down to us.

We remember our great ancestor the Earth and her great ancestor the universe itself.

"Ancient buddhas and ancestors were as we; we shall come to be buddhas and ancestors. Venerating buddhas and ancestors, we are one with buddhas and ancestors; contemplating awakened mind, we are one with awakened mind."[27]

Written by Kaspa and the Healing Oppression Group of Extinction Rebellion Buddhists.

Appendix E: Meal time and incense offering verses

Four meal time verses

Infinite benefits bless the breakfast food,
all beings profit greatly therefrom
Since the results are limitless and wonderful,
the pleasure is ours for eternity.
*

This food is the gift of the whole universe:
the earth, the sky, all sentient beings.
In this food is much joy, much suffering, much hard work.
We accept this food so that we may follow the path of
    practice,
and help all beings everywhere.
*

The first bite is to cut off delusion,
the second bite is to grow in faith,
the third bite is to help all beings.
We pray that all may be enlightened.
We pray for peace in this world,
and the cessation of all misfortune.

*

The Buddha invites us to eat in mindfulness,
of the food, the earth, the world around us.
We pray that our minds may not become dull,
nor our attention scattered,
and that we may realize the deep significance of life.

Incense offerings

From Plum Village
In gratitude we offer this incense
to all buddhas and bodhisattvas
throughout space and time.
May it be as fragrant as earth herself
reflecting our careful efforts,
our whole-hearted mindfulness,
and the fruit of understanding
slowly ripening.
May we and all beings be
companions of buddhas and bodhisattvas,
May we awaken from forgetfulness,
and realise out True Home

From Amida Shu
The fragrance of this incense
permeates our practice centre,
and goes forth to worlds beyond.
In the sincerity of our training
the Sanghakaya is revealed.
Hearts and minds bow in gratitude.
Offerings multiply like the action,
of the all good one,
and the light that knows no obstacle
fills the Dharma realm.

Glossary

Amida Buddha – the Buddha of unlimited light and unlimited life. Shakyamuni Buddha told the story of Amida Buddha who existed in Shakyamuni's distant past.

Avalokiteshvara (Sanskrit) – the Sanskrit word for Quan Shi Yin, the Bodhisattva of Compassion.

Bodhisattva (Sanskrit) – Bodhisattvas are inspired by the buddhas and, although not yet buddhas themselves, have great compassion and dedicate themselves to helping all sentient beings.

Bombu (Japanese) – a foolish being of wayward passion (i.e. all of us). As bombu beings we put ourselves in relationship with Amida Buddha and trust that if we say the nembutsu our rebirth in the Pure Land is guaranteed.

Buddha (Sanskrit) – an enlightened being. Often used to mean Shakyamuni Buddha, the historical Buddha, who lived in India 2500 years ago.

Contrition – a deep feeling of regret and sadness that arises when we fully realise the harmful consequence of our actions, whether intended or otherwise. Not to be confused with 'beating ourselves up' which is when self-protective parts of us shame us to try and protect us from being judged or rejected again.

Dharma (Sanskrit) – The teachings of the Buddha. Also sometimes used to mean 'things as they are' or 'what is true'. One of the three jewels.

Dharmakara (Sanskrit) – the king in the Larger Pure Land Sutra – the story Shakyamuni Buddha told to Ananda when Ananda noticed he was glowing. Dharmakara was inspired by the Buddha Lokeshvararaja and went on to eventually become Amida Buddha.

Dukkha (Sanskrit) – the Sanskrit word used to mean affliction or suffering. The first of the four noble truths.

The four noble truths – the first teaching the Buddha gave and one that he repeated through the decades of his Dharma.

Honen Shonin – (1133–1212) Japanese Buddhist sage, and founder of Jodo Shu, the first Independent Pure Land school in Japan.

Jodo Shu (Japanese) – the school of Buddhism founded by Honen Shonin.

Jodo Shinshu (Japanese) – the school of Buddhism founded by Shinran Shonin, one of Honen's disciples. Currently the largest Pure Land school in Japan.

Karma (Sanskrit) – the Buddhist idea that intentional action sows seeds that ripen in the future, either as internal mental states or worldly circumstance.

Lokeshvararaja (Sanskrit) – the Buddha encountered by Dharmakara and who inspired him to take his vows and become Amida Buddha.

Mahayana Buddhism – one of the main two branches of Buddhism (the other is Theravada) practised widely in China, Japan, Korea, Tibet and Taiwan. Made up of a collection of Buddhist schools including Zen, Tibetan and Pure Land Buddhism.

Minister – a fully ordained priest in the Bright Earth Buddhist Order.

Namo Amida Bu – the nembutsu – saying the name of Amida Buddha. In Japan they say Namu Amida Butsu, and in China they say Namo Omito Fo.

Nembutsu (Japanese) – the practice of saying 'Namo Amida Bu'. In the Larger Pure Land Sutra it says that anyone who hears the name of Amida Buddha will be reborn in his Pure Land. Honen asks us to recite the nembutsu so it is audible to our own ears.

Pali – the language in which the scriptures of the Theravada School of Buddhism are recorded.

Precepts – ethical ideals such as 'do not take life' which we aspire to as Buddhists.

The Pure Land – generally, in Pure Land Buddhism, this refers to the realm of bliss that surrounds Amida Buddha. This is described in great detail in the Larger Pure Land Sutra as a place where there are cool pools of bathing water, jewelled trees, beautiful melodious music etc. Some Pure Land Buddhists see the Pure Land as a real place where they will be reborn after death, or as a metaphor for what happens to us when we die. Others see it as a vision of an ideal society where we care for each other and the environment, and which we can start working towards right now in this life.

Pure Land Buddhism – the form of Buddhism popularised by Honen in the 12th century in Japan, based on the vows made by Amida Buddha.

Quan Shi Yin (Chinese) – the Bodhisattva of Compassion, also known as Avalokiteshvara.

Refuge – taking refuge is a central practice for all Buddhists and gives us a sense of security and faith. Most Buddhists take refuge in the three jewels – Shakyamuni Buddha, the Dharma and the Sangha.

Rupa (Sanskrit) – the power that an object has to draw our attention, or an object that is highly charged with personal meaning. We also speak of Buddha statues as being 'Buddha rupas' as they represent the Buddha.

Samadhi (Sanskrit) – a state of peaceful concentration or consummate vision.

Samsara (Sanskrit) – the continuing cycle of birth and death, the world of karma, and the worldly world.

Sange-mon (Japanese) – can be translated as the 'gate of contrition', which we all need to walk through in order to find grace. A genuine experience of our limitations and failings points us towards Amida Buddha, who accepts us just as we are.

Sangha (Sanskrit) – the community of people who follow the Buddha's teachings. One of the three jewels.

Sanskrit – the primary language used by Indian Mahayana Buddhists.

Shakyamuni Buddha (Sanskrit) – literally 'sage of the Shakyas'. The Buddha (born as a prince, Siddhartha Gautama) who lived 2500 years ago in India and who founded Buddhism as a religion.

Shinjin – An experience of settled faith which we receive when we say the nembutsu without any need to manipulate what we receive in return.

Shinran – A disciple of Honen's who went on to found the Jodo Shinshu school of Pure Land Buddhism in Japan – the largest existing school of Pure Land Buddhism today.

Sukhavati (Sanskrit) – another word for the Pure Land. Literally 'sweet or blissful land'.

Sutra (Sanskrit) – the sacred scriptures that contain the discourses of the Buddha (sutta in Pali).

Theravada Buddhism – literally 'path of the elders'. The branch of Buddhism which uses the teachings of the Pali Canon. The dominant religion in Sri Lanka, Thailand, Cambodia and Laos and with practitioners across the world.

The Three Jewels – what all Buddhists take refuge in – the Buddha, the Dharma and the Sangha.

Zazen (Japanese) – Zen meditation practice. Often 'just sitting' where you sit upright and quietly on a zafu (a meditation cushion) without putting energy into anything else (thinking, for example).

Further reading

What follows is a mix of recommended Pure Land and other Buddhist texts and our personal favourite books. This is a good essay to start with:

'What is Amida' by Nobuo Haneda:
https://seattlebetsuin.com/what_is_amida_buddha.htm

In addition to these Buddhist books, we recommend that all of our Sangha become familiar with Internal Family Systems either by reading Parts Work by Tom Holmes (an easy introduction) or No Bad Parts, the introduction to IFS by its founder Richard Schwartz.

Atone, Joji *The Promise of Amida's Buddha: Honen's Path to Bliss* (2011) Wisdom Publications

Bloom, Alfred *Essential Shinran: The Path of True Entrusting* (2006) World Wisdom Books

Bikkhu Bodhi (Translator) *The Connected Discourses of the Buddha: A Translation of the Samyutta Nikaya* (2003) Wisdom Publications

Bikkhu Bodhi (Translator) *The Numerical Discourses of the Buddha: A Complete Translation of the Anguttara Nikaya (Teachings of the Buddha)* (2012) Wisdom Publications

Brazier, Caroline *The Other Buddhism: Amida Comes West* (2007) O Books

Brazier, David *The Feeling Buddha: A Buddhist Psychology of Character, Adversity and Passion* (2002) Robinson

Fitzgerald, Joseph A. *Honen the Buddhist Saint: Essential Writings and Official Biography* (2006) World Wisdom Books

Haneda, Nobuo *Dharma Breeze: Essays on Shin Buddhism* (2020) Maida Center of Buddhism

Jones, Charles B. *Pure Land History Tradition and Practice* (2021) Shambhala Publications

Keenan, Terrance *Zen Encounters With Loneliness* (2014) Wisdom Publications

Keown, Damien *Buddhism: A Very Short Introduction* (2013) OUP Oxford

Kornfield, Jack *After the Ecstasy, the Laundry* (2000) Rider

Kubose, Gyomay *The Center Within* (2009) Stone Bridge Press

Kubose, Gyomay *Everyday Suchness* (2004) Stone Bridge Press

Manuel, Zenju Earthlyn *The Way of Tenderness: Awakening through Race, Sexuality, and Gender* (2014) Wisdom Publications

Nagapriya *The Promise of a Sacred World: Shinran's Teaching of Other Power* (2022) Windhorse Publications

Bikkhu Nanamoli (Translator) Bikkhu Bodhi (Translator) *The Middle Length Discourses of the Buddha: A Translation of the Majjhima Nikaya (Teachings of the Buddha)* (1995) Wisdom Publications

Paraskevopoulos, John *Call of the Infinite: The Way of Shin Buddhism* (2009) Sophia Perennis et Universalis

Robyn, Satya *Coming Home: Refuge in Pure Land Buddhism* (2019) Woodsmoke Press

Shapiro, Rami *Recovery – The Sacred Art: The Twelve Steps as Spiritual Practice* (2009) Skylight Paths Publishing

Shigaraki, Takamaro *Heart of the Shin Buddhist Path: A Life of Awakening* (2013) Wisdom Publications

Suzuki, Shunryu *Zen Mind, Beginner's Mind* (2005) Weatherhill

Unno, Taitetsu *Shin Buddhism: Bits of Rubble Turn into Gold* (2002) Harmony

Unno, Taitetsu *River of Fire, River of Water* (1998) Image

Welwood, John *Toward a Psychology of Awakening: Buddhism, Psychotherapy, and the Path of Personal and Spiritual Transformation* (2002) Shambhala

Wilson, Jeff *Living Nembutsu: Applying Shinran's Radically Engaged Buddhism in Life and Society* (2023) The Sumeru Press

Walshe, Maurice (Translator), Sumedho, Ajahn (Foreword) *The Long Discourses of the Buddha: A Translation of the Digha Nikaya* (1995) Wisdom Publications

NOTES

[1] Van de Wetering, J. *A Glimpse of Nothingness*, St Martin's Griffin 1999

[2] Roshi P.T.N.H. Jiyu-Kennett, *The Wild White Goose*, Shasta Abbey Buddhist Supplies, 2002

[3] The Moon Cannot be Stolen, accessed 1/11/15
http://truecenterpublishing.com/zenstory/moon.html

[4] McMahan, David L *Modernity and the Discourse of Scientific Buddhism*, Journal of the American Academy of Religion 72, no. 4 (2004): 897–933

[5] Ford, James, *Spilling the Beans: Or, what I learned by living for seventy-five years*, accessed 18/10/23
https://www.patheos.com/blogs/monkeymind/2023/07/spilling-the-beans-or-what-i-learned-by-living-for-seventy-five-years.html

[6] Schwartz, Dr. Richard quoted in *No Bad Parts*, accessed 18/10/23
https://internalfamilysystems.pt/multimedia/webinars/no-bad-parts-individual-and-collective-healing-dick-schwartz

[7] Rev Kubose, Koyo speaking on *Everyday Buddhism Episode 2: A Bright Dawn* https://www.everyday-buddhism.com/everyday-buddhism-20-a-bright-dawn-conversation-with-rev-koyo-kubose/ accessed 23/11/23

[8] Hamilton Panting, Camille, *The Golden Chain*
https://www.lionsroar.com/the-golden-chain-guide-to-a-life-of-love accessed 31/10/23

[9] Palmer, Amanda *The Art of Asking* (2014) Grand Central Publishing

[10] Shinran Tr Inagaki, Hisao *Kyogyoshinsho* (2003) BDK & Numata Center

[11] Nouwen, Henri J. M. *Life of the Beloved* (2002) Better Yourself Books

[12] Lamott, Anne *Traveling Mercies: Some Thoughts on Faith* (2000) Anchor Books

[13]Guyette, Angelle *Small Victories: Anne Lamott writes about grace for those who hate books about grace* Pittsburgh Post–Gazette Dec 21 2014

[14]Smith C. Wilfred, quoted in Tanaka, Kenneth, *OCEAN* http://www.yamadera.info/ocean/ocean-index.htm accessed 25/10/23

[15]Palmer, Amanda *The Art of Asking* (2014) Grand Central Publishing

[16]Loori, John Daido *Mountain Record of Zen Talks* (1988) Shambhala Publications

[17]Samyutta Nikaya 47.19

[18]*Shantideva Guide to the Bodhisattva's Way of Life* Tr. Gyatso, Kelsang (2002) Tharpa Publications

[19] Matthew 11:30

[20] See 13

[21]Rogers, Carl R. *On Becoming a Person* (2004) Robinson

[22]Quoted in Bate, Walter Jackson *John Keats* (1964) Belknap Press

[23]Gyonen *The Essentials of the Vinaya Tradition and The Collected Teachings of the Tendai Lotus School* Tr. Pruden, Leo and Swanson, Paul (1995) BDK America

[24]Samyutta Nikaya 45.2

[25] Lief, Judith *Bowing* Tricycle (Fall 1994)

[26] https://brightdawn.org/Everyday%20Gassho.pdf

[27] From Eihei Koso Hotsuganmon

Milton Keynes UK
Ingram Content Group UK Ltd.
UKHW020800250224
438379UK00013B/1388